Charlottesville

A CONTEMPORARY PORTRAIT

Charlottesville Regional Chamber of Commerce

The Charlottesville Regional Chamber of Commerce and Community Communications, Inc. would like to express our gratitude to those companies for their leadership in the development of this book.

Library of Congress Cataloging-in-Publication Data

DiMaggio, Joanne, 1950-
  Charlottesville : a contemporary portrait / by Joanne DiMaggio ; featuring the photography of Philip Beaurline.—1st ed.
      p. cm.
  ISBN 1-58192-045-8
  1. Charlottesville Region (Va.)—Civilization. 2. Charlottesville Region (Va.)—Pictorial works. 3. Charlottesville Region (Va.)—Economic conditions. 4. Business enterprises—Virginia—Charlottesville Region. I. Title.
  F234.C47 D56 2001
  975.5'481—dc21
                              2001008738

Charlottesville

A CONTEMPORARY PORTRAIT

By Joanne DiMaggio • Editorial Coordination by Karen Haley
Featuring the photography of Philip Beaurline

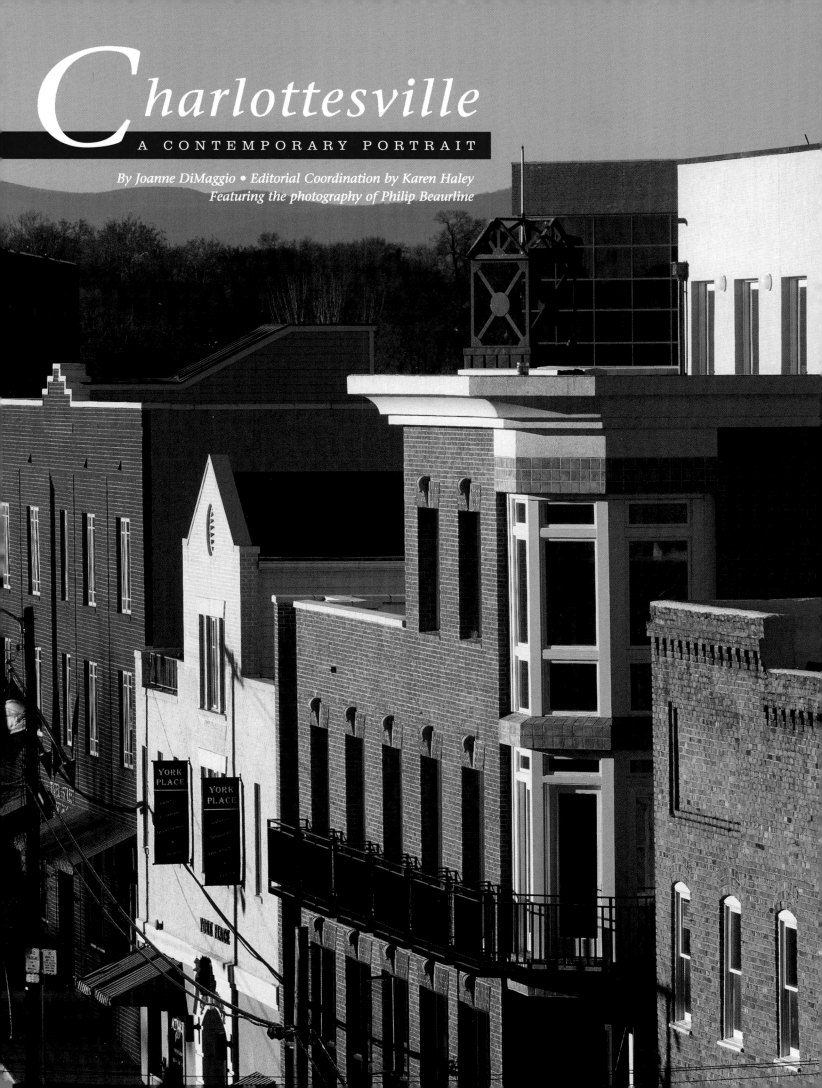

Charlottesville: A Contemporary Portrait

By Joanne DiMaggio
Editorial Coordination by Karen Haley
Featuring the photography of Philip Beaurline

Community Communications, Inc.
Publisher: Ronald P. Beers

Charlottesville Regional
Chamber of Commerce

Charlottesville Regional Chamber of Commerce
President, Editor: Timothy Hulbert
Project Manager, Editor: Laurence Banner

Staff for *Charlottesville: A Contemporary Portrait*
Acquisitions: Henry Beers
Publisher's Sales Associate: Jim Sparks
Editor in Chief: Wendi Lewis
Managing Editor: Kurt R. Niland
Profile Editors: Amanda J. Burbank and Jim Dunham
Editorial Assistants: Beth Beasley
Design Director: Scott Phillips
Designer: Matt Johnson
Photo Editors: Kurt R. Niland and Matt Johnson
Pre-Press and Separations: Artcraft Graphic Productions
National Sales Manager: Keely Smith
Sales Assistants: Brandon Maddox and Annette Lozier
Accounting Services: Stephanie Perez

CCI

Community Communications, Inc.
Montgomery, Alabama

David M. Williamson, Chief Executive Officer
Ronald P. Beers, President
W. David Brown, Chief Operating Officer

PHOTO BY PHILIP BEAURLINE

COVER PHOTO BY PHILIP BEAURLINE

TABLE OF CONTENTS
■ ■ ■ ■ ■

1 | CHAPTER **ONE**
Life in The Charlottesville Region: An American Dream, *12*

"Life is of no value but as it brings us gratifications. Among the most valuable of these is rational society. It informs the mind, sweetens the temper, cheers our spirits, and promotes health."
— *Thomas Jefferson, Letter to James Madison, 1784*

2 | CHAPTER **TWO**
Charlottesville History: A Bridge In Time, *30*

"A morsel of genuine history is a thing so rare as to be always valuable."
— *Thomas Jefferson, Letter to John Adams, 1817*

3 | CHAPTER **THREE**
A Strong, Diversified Economy, *38*

"Agriculture, manufactures, commerce, and navigation, the four pillars of our prosperity, are the most thriving when left most free to individual enterprise."
— *Thomas Jefferson, First Annual Presidential Message, 1801*

4 | CHAPTER **FOUR**
A Cradle For High-Tech Visionaries, *48*

"Where a new invention is supported by well known principles, and promises to be useful, it ought to be tried."
— *Thomas Jefferson, Letter to Robert Fulton, 1810*

5 | CHAPTER **FIVE**
A Mecca For The Arts, *54*

"I am an enthusiast on the subject of the arts. But it is an enthusiasm of which I am not ashamed, as its object is to improve the taste of my countrymen, to increase their reputation, to reconcile them to the respect of the world, and procure them its praise."
— *Thomas Jefferson, Letter to James Madison, 1785*

6 | CHAPTER **SIX**
Education: A Vision For Leadership, *64*

"No other sure foundation can be devised for the preservation of freedom and happiness."
— *Thomas Jefferson, Letter to George Wythe, 1786*

7 | CHAPTER **SEVEN**
Health Care-Simply The Best, *74*

"Without health there is no happiness. An attention to health, then, should take place of every other object."
— *Thomas Jefferson, Letter to T.M. Randolph, Jr., 1787*

8 | CHAPTER **EIGHT**
The Future of the Charlottesville Region, *80*

"I like the dreams of the future better than the history of the past."
— *Thomas Jefferson, Letter to John Adams, 1816*

PHOTO BY PHILIP BEAURLINE

FOREWORD

"Charlottesville"—throughout the Commonwealth of Virginia and beyond, that one word evokes a uniquely positive, vibrant, dynamic, verdant portrait in the minds of almost everyone who hears it.

Charlottesville and its distinctive surrounding region is often described boldly within our own community as "the cultural and historical center of Thomas Jefferson's Virginia."

Our Charlottesville Regional Chamber of Commerce is pleased to present this handsome book, *Charlottesville: A Contemporary Portrait*.

This "portrait" focuses on a part of our community's natural environment, heritage, dynamic economy, culture, educational excellence, and is followed by profiles of a number of Chamber businesses and civic organizations, which together help power the economic engine that drives much of this success.

Charlottesville: A Contemporary Portrait is the result of the effort of a number of creative people including our author Joanne DiMaggio; editorial coordinator Karen Haley; our photographer Philip Beaurline; and Henry Beers, Kurt Niland, and Jim Sparks—the publishing team at Community Communications Inc., our Chamber partners in this venture.

Charlottesville: A Contemporary Portrait came to be from the vision and hard work of our Charlottesville Regional Chamber of Commerce—notably our Board of Directors led by 2000 Chairman Robert Moorefield, 2001 Chairman Tom Grinde, 2002 Chairman Michael Gaffney, Jane Dittmar, who served as our Chamber's President and chief executive for the decade leading into 2001, our Chamber staff, and the Chamber member businesses and civic organizations who actively supported the exciting project.

Throughout, Larry Banner's steady dedication and effort ensured that *Charlottesville: A Contemporary Portrait* would be an excellent publication. As our Chamber Project Manager and Managing Editor, Larry developed and delivered this unique, impressive Chamber achievement.

Together we trust you will enjoy *Charlottesville: A Contemporary Portrait* and our greater Charlottesville communities.

Thank you.

Timothy Hulbert
President

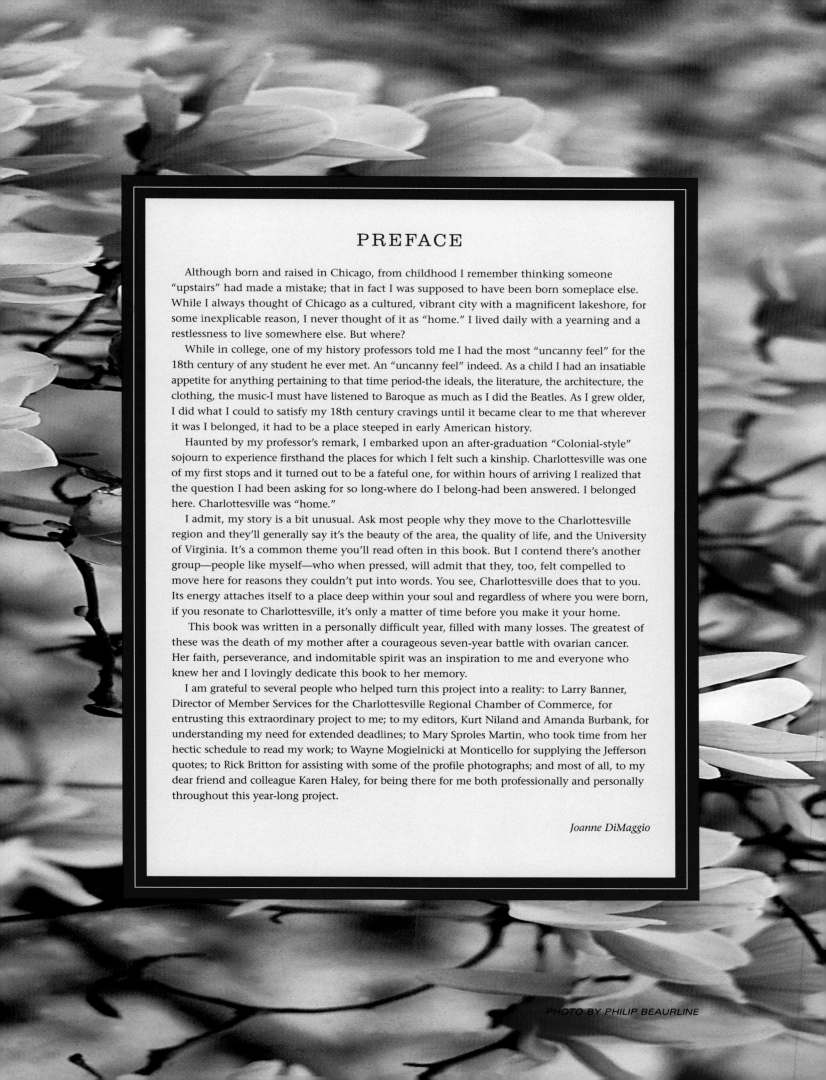

PREFACE

Although born and raised in Chicago, from childhood I remember thinking someone "upstairs" had made a mistake; that in fact I was supposed to have been born someplace else. While I always thought of Chicago as a cultured, vibrant city with a magnificent lakeshore, for some inexplicable reason, I never thought of it as "home." I lived daily with a yearning and a restlessness to live somewhere else. But where?

While in college, one of my history professors told me I had the most "uncanny feel" for the 18th century of any student he ever met. An "uncanny feel" indeed. As a child I had an insatiable appetite for anything pertaining to that time period-the ideals, the literature, the architecture, the clothing, the music-I must have listened to Baroque as much as I did the Beatles. As I grew older, I did what I could to satisfy my 18th century cravings until it became clear to me that wherever it was I belonged, it had to be a place steeped in early American history.

Haunted by my professor's remark, I embarked upon an after-graduation "Colonial-style" sojourn to experience firsthand the places for which I felt such a kinship. Charlottesville was one of my first stops and it turned out to be a fateful one, for within hours of arriving I realized that the question I had been asking for so long-where do I belong-had been answered. I belonged here. Charlottesville was "home."

I admit, my story is a bit unusual. Ask most people why they move to the Charlottesville region and they'll generally say it's the beauty of the area, the quality of life, and the University of Virginia. It's a common theme you'll read often in this book. But I contend there's another group—people like myself—who when pressed, will admit that they, too, felt compelled to move here for reasons they couldn't put into words. You see, Charlottesville does that to you. Its energy attaches itself to a place deep within your soul and regardless of where you were born, if you resonate to Charlottesville, it's only a matter of time before you make it your home.

This book was written in a personally difficult year, filled with many losses. The greatest of these was the death of my mother after a courageous seven-year battle with ovarian cancer. Her faith, perseverance, and indomitable spirit was an inspiration to me and everyone who knew her and I lovingly dedicate this book to her memory.

I am grateful to several people who helped turn this project into a reality: to Larry Banner, Director of Member Services for the Charlottesville Regional Chamber of Commerce, for entrusting this extraordinary project to me; to my editors, Kurt Niland and Amanda Burbank, for understanding my need for extended deadlines; to Mary Sproles Martin, who took time from her hectic schedule to read my work; to Wayne Mogielnicki at Monticello for supplying the Jefferson quotes; to Rick Britton for assisting with some of the profile photographs; and most of all, to my dear friend and colleague Karen Haley, for being there for me both professionally and personally throughout this year-long project.

Joanne DiMaggio

LIFE IN THE CHARLOTTESVILLE REGION: AN AMERICAN DREAM

......

"Life is of no value but as it brings us gratifications. Among the most valuable of these is rational society. It informs the mind, sweetens the temper, cheers our spirits, and promotes health."

—Thomas Jefferson
Letter to James Madison, 1784

IT'S EASY TO FALL IN LOVE WITH CHARLOTTESVILLE. FRAMED BY EXTRAORDINARY MOUNTAIN VIEWS AND WINDING COUNTRY ROADS, THE AREA IS A REFUGE FOR THOSE WHO PREFER TO LIVE AMID NATURAL SURROUNDINGS.
PHOTO BY PHILIP BEAURLINE

Every generation seeks a lifestyle that is better than the one enjoyed by previous generations. Better housing in solid, safe neighborhoods. Better educational opportunities. Better career options. Better social and recreational outlets. Better physical surroundings. Doing "better" is part of the American credo, so it isn't surprising that people are choosing to relocate to areas based on the quality of life factor. And it's those three words-quality of life-that are a leading reason people from all over the world choose to live and work in the Charlottesville region.

It's easy to fall in love with Charlottesville. Framed by extraordinary mountain views and winding country roads, the area is a refuge for those who prefer to live amid natural surroundings, yet still have access to the culture, attractions, and activities traditionally associated with a more urban area. The Charlottesville region is a rare combination of both.

Situated in the eastern foothills of the Blue Ridge Mountains some 70 miles west of Richmond and 110 miles southwest of Washington, DC, the area enjoys mild winters averaging 37 degrees, and mild but humid summers averaging 75 degrees.

The City of Charlottesville is the heart of the region. It has an autonomous, independent municipal government. As the seat of both the City of Charlottesville and Albemarle County governments, Charlottesville serves as the economic, cultural, and educational center of a multi-county region in Central Virginia, which also includes the counties of Greene, Orange, Nelson, Fluvanna, Madison, and Louisa.

The Charlottesville region consistently has ranked high in quality of life standards because of its enviable health care systems, affordable housing, low crime, low unemployment, cultural and social amenities, outstanding schools with high educational standards, and convenient transportation outlets.

Recent accolades include Arts & Entertainment Television, which listed Charlottesville as #6 in its Top 10 Cities to Have It All. The Searchers, an independent organization providing information to retired persons, awarded Charlottesville an Outstanding Community Award for 2000. *Modern Maturity* Magazine placed Charlottesville as #2 under College Towns in its list of 50 Most Alive Places to Live. In 1998, *Money* Magazine named Charlottesville as the #1 Small City in the South. In 1997, *Golf Digest* rated Charlottesville as the #1 Best Golf Community for Retirees. That same year the American Association of State Climatologists said Charlottesville had the #2 Best Climate on the East Coast; *Tennis Magazine* named Charlottesville its #1 Tennis Community; *Reader's Digest* listed it as the #7

THE FALL FOLIAGE IN CHARLOTTESVILLE IS TRULY BREATHTAKING. BRILLIANT YELLOWS AND FIERY REDS PROUDLY ANNOUNCE THAT AUTUMN HAS ARRIVED. WITH ITS MANY WARM, RICH COLORS, IT'S NO WONDER THAT THE LANDSCAPE IS THE INSPIRATION FOR LOCAL ARTISTS.
PHOTO BY PHILIP BEAURLINE

Best Place to Raise A Family; and *Point of View* deemed Charlottesville its #7 Best City to Start a Business. The list goes on and on and deservedly so. With such high praise, impressive statistics, and global exposure, it's no wonder that people from virtually everywhere in the world come to Charlottesville seeking a better life for themselves and their families.

Out of the many reasons to move to the Charlottesville region, the area's natural beauty and aesthetics are mentioned most often. Within the breathtaking Blue Ridge Mountains, just west of Charlottesville, is Shenandoah National Park, which features numerous trails for hiking and backpacking. For those who prefer a leisurely drive, the Skyline Drive and the Blue Ridge Parkway offer some of the most spectacular overlooks in the country, especially during the fall when autumn leaves display a brilliant burst of fiery colors.

The Blue Ridge Mountains also are home to one of Virginia's premier four-season resorts. Located in Nelson County and a favorite getaway for locals is Wintergreen Resort. Consisting of 11,000 acres of which more than 6,000 acres have been preserved as undisturbed wilderness, Wintergreen was named one of the "best examples of ecofriendly development in the United States" by *Hemispheres* magazine. Wintergreen is known for its championship golf courses, nationally acclaimed tennis programs, and some of the country's best skiing and snowboarding slopes and trails. This world-class resort also features hiking and biking trails, horseback riding, fishing and boating, tubing, a luxurious spa, fine dining facilities, nature and cultural programs, music festivals, and is a popular conference and meeting center.

County parks throughout the Charlottesville region offer convenient, affordable vacation alternatives. With 62 water acres, two of which are beach acres, Chris Greene Lake Park is Albemarle County's most popular summer swimming spot. Picturesque Mint Springs Valley Park is surrounded by mountains on three sides and features 512 acres with nature trails that meander over old mountain roads. Albemarle County's biggest park, Walnut Creek, is known for its mountain bike trails. The 104-acre Beaver Creek Lake is considered the largest and best fishing lake in Albemarle County. And of course, there's the James River, where each year thousands of people come to fish or to leisurely float downstream in an inner tube, on a raft, or in a canoe. A popular annual event on this historic river is The James River Batteau Festival, honoring the flat-bottomed boats that were used to transport tobacco from areas of Central Virginia to Richmond during the late 1700s.

Darden Towe Memorial Park, located off Route 20 North, is the primary athletic field complex in the area, featuring softball fields, multi-purpose fields used

CHARLOTTESVILLE IS SURROUNDED BY RURAL VISTAS, MOUNTAIN PANORAMAS, AND PASTORAL COMFORTS, MAKING IT EASY FOR CITY DWELLERS TO ESCAPE THE PRESSURES OF EVERYDAY LIFE WITH JUST A SHORT DRIVE. *PHOTO BY PHILIP BEAURLINE*

for soccer, lacrosse and football, tennis courts, a running trail, children's play area, picnic shelter, grilling area, and access to the Rivanna River. McIntire Park, on Route 250, has swimming, shelters, a playground, athletic fields, golf and tennis facilities. And Pen Park on Rio Road offers hiking, shelters, playground, athletic fields, jogging trail, golf and tennis. Other recreational activities available in the Charlottesville region include the Charlottesville Ice Park, bowling alleys, tennis courts, indoor and outdoor swimming pools, miniature golf, numerous fitness centers, and a selection of country clubs.

The region is blessed with several unspoiled natural areas that have been set aside for study and exploration. Ivy Creek in Albemarle County is a 215-acre natural area of pine and hardwood forests, old fields, streams, natural springs, and walking trails. The Ragged Mountain Natural Area features 980 acres of undisturbed land surrounding Albemarle County's Ragged Mountain Reservoir. Here visitors can observe and study nature, hike, and fish. The Hardware Wildlife Management Area in Fluvanna County encompasses more than 1,000 acres, including the 50-acre Fluvanna-Ruritan Lake. And at 13,000 acres, Lake Anna in Louisa County's Lake Anna State Park, is the second largest lake in Virginia.

THE CHARLOTTESVILLE REGION IS BLESSED WITH SEVERAL UNSPOILED NATURAL AREAS THAT HAVE BEEN SET ASIDE FOR STUDY, EXPLORATION, AND PRESERVATION. RESIDENTS AND VISITORS ENJOY ACRES OF PINE AND HARDWOOD FORESTS, OLD FIELDS, STREAMS, NATURAL SPRINGS, AND WALKING TRAILS. *PHOTO BY PHILIP BEAURLINE*

Recognized by *Golf Digest* as a superb golfing destination, the Charlottesville region has a number of public and private golf courses within the city and surrounding counties. For a distinctive golf experience, Wintergreen features Devils Knob, the highest course in Virginia at nearly 4,000 feet; and the nationally-ranked Stoney Creek course, featuring 27 holes designed by world-renowned golf course architect, Rees Jones.

Virginia is equestrian country and some of the finest hunt clubs are located in the area. Fox hunting, polo matches, and horse shows are held throughout the region. The most popular equestrian events are the Foxfield Races, held in Albemarle County, and the Montpelier Races that take place on the grounds of Montpelier, home of James Madison in Orange County. Each locale hosts fall and spring races that are enormously popular with local and visiting equestrian enthusiasts.

Who knew more about wine than Thomas Jefferson? Therefore, it is only fitting that today the Charlottesville region is known for having some of the most famous wineries and vineyards in the world. Designated for its unique wine-growing conditions, the Monticello viticultural area is one of six nationally recognized areas in the state and is considered the Wine Capital of Virginia. Most wineries hold daily tours and tastings, and many sponsor special events. Some of the more popular wineries include Jefferson Vineyards, White Hall Vineyards, and Oakencroft Winery in Albemarle County; Mountain Cove Vineyards in Nelson County; Prince Michel Vineyards in Madison County; and Barboursville Vineyards and Horton Cellars in Orange County.

Festivals abound in the Charlottesville region. In mid-April, the Annual Dogwood Festival ushers in spring with festivities that include a parade and carnival rides. The Crozet Arts & Crafts Festival in early May showcases the work of some of the most talented artisans in the region. People from all over the country come to Charlottesville to participate in the nationally acclaimed Virginia Festival of the Book and the Virginia Film Festival. Another annual event that draws people from across the states is Historic Garden Week, when many of the private and historic estates in the region open their gates to visitors who enjoy the spectacular color, fragrance, and design of some of the area's most exquisite gardens.

The hills surrounding the Charlottesville area are definitely alive with the sound of music. Music festivals, concerts, orchestral performances, operas, local pop and folk bands, perform under the sky from April through October. The University of Virginia provides area residents with an assortment of cultural and entertainment activities, including theatrical performances, concerts, lectures, and museum exhibits. Similarly, many

SEVERAL PARKS WITHIN THE CITY PROVIDE OUTDOOR AREAS FOR FAMILY OUTINGS, PICNICS, AFTER-WORK STROLLS, AND OTHER OPPORTUNITIES TO TRADE CITY PAVEMENT FOR GREEN SPACES. *PHOTO BY PHILIP BEAURLINE*

community organizations offer a sophisticated cultural calendar with programs ranging from symphony orchestras to children's theater.

The Charlottesville region has been home to patriots and presidents. Rich in both famous and lesser-known historic treasures, the area has been a cradle for democracy, nurturing leaders who created the American dream and then turned it into a reality. From Monticello to Ash Lawn-Highland, Michie Tavern, Montpelier, the University of Virginia, Court Square, and hundreds of historic locales between, residents and visitors alike are able to step back into time and learn firsthand about the lives and accomplishments of the area's most influential eighteenth and nineteenth century personalities.

Museums play an important role in contributing to the quality of life in Charlottesville. One of the most popular is the Virginia Discovery Museum. Located on the East End of the Downtown Mall, the Virginia Discovery Museum is a hands-on children's museum, with exhibits on the arts, sciences, humanities, history, and nature. The Frontier Culture Museum in the Shenandoah Valley brings the past alive with four farms with their furnishings, gardens, animals, crops, and costumed interpreters, creating a living history of life as it was in Europe and America during the seventeenth, eighteenth, and nineteenth centuries. Walton's Mountain Museum, located in Schuyler, Virginia, contains exhibits of rooms and memorabilia from the set of the television series, *The Waltons*.

WHILE EMBRACING GROWTH, CHARLOTTESVILLE ALSO PRIZES ITS SMALL-TOWN APPEAL. DOWNTOWN STREETS LINED WITH SMALL SHOPS AND CAFES POSSESS A CASUAL CHARM-A SIMPLE ENHANCEMENT TO EVERYDAY LIFE FOR ALL CITY DWELLERS. *PHOTO BY PHILIP BEAURLINE*

FOUR DISTINCT SEASONS GRACE CHARLOTTESVILLE WITH NATURAL SPLENDOR AND EVER-CHANGING SCENERY. ABOVE: SPRING, NATURE'S OPENING ACT, IS CHARACTERIZED BY MILD WARMTH AND THE BRILLIANT COLORS OF FLOWERS AND BUDDING TREES EVERYWHERE. BELOW: THE WARM, HUMID DAYS OF MID-SUMMER SLOW THE PACE OF DAILY LIFE JUST ENOUGH, WHILE LURING RESIDENTS OUTDOORS TO ENJOY THE AREA'S LUSH GREEN LANDSCAPES. *PHOTOS BY PHIL BEAURLINE*

Coffeehouses, dining establishments, cinemas, and shopping are plentiful throughout the Charlottesville region. Students and retirees alike frequent the many quaint coffeehouses that can be found virtually everywhere, from the Corner at the University of Virginia, to shopping areas interspersed throughout Charlottesville neighborhoods. The same is true of area cinemas, showing everything from the latest blockbusters to vintage classics. Gourmet restaurants, pancake houses, country inns, historic taverns, and ethnic specialty houses provide a variety of culinary delights sure to please every palate. And for shoppers, there is the incomparable selection of specialty shops at Barracks Road, and the variety of famous-name retail stores that line the Fashion Square Mall.

To get a real feel for the uniqueness of Charlottesville, however, a stroll along the Downtown Mall is a must. This pedestrian mall offers visitors an afternoon of pleasant surprises with its vast assortment of specialty shops, variety stores, restaurants, galleries, and entertainment. The Mall is a favorite gathering place for special events held throughout the year. From "Fridays After Five", where local bands play to enthusiastic audiences during warm-weather months; to First Night Virginia, where Charlottesville families welcome the New Year in a safe and fun-filled environment; to every historic program and holiday event in between, the Downtown Mall epitomizes the spirit of the Charlottesville community.

For those fortunate souls who call the Charlottesville region home, there is an abundance of resources that make life in this area so worthwhile. With all the amenities of a large city, yet retaining the warmth and charm of a small town, the Charlottesville area continues to attract men and women of all ages who are seeking a better way of life that is, and always has been, an American Dream. ■

ABOVE: CRISP AUTUMN AIR, FIERY FOLIAGE, AND THE SPICY FRAGRANCE OF LEAVES AND PUMPKIN PIE ARE THE HALLMARKS OF A PERFECT AUTUMN IN CHARLOTTESVILLE, MAKING IT MANY A RESIDENT'S FAVORITE SEASON. BELOW: WINTER IN CHARLOTTESVILLE OFTEN ARRIVES COLD AND SNOWY, BUT NEVER OVERSTAYS ITS WELCOME. JUST ADD A BLANKET OF FRESH SNOW, AND THE LOCAL GEOGRAPHY BECOMES A SKIER'S AND SLEDDER'S PARADISE. *PHOTOS BY PHILIP BEAURLINE*

OUTDOOR ENTHUSIASTS ARE HAPPY TO CALL THE CHARLOTTESVILLE AREA HOME. CANOEING, SWIMMING, HIKING, BIKING, PICNICKING, SKIING, SKATING, SLEDDING, AND HUNDREDS OF OTHER RECREATIONAL OPPORTUNITIES PROVIDED BY MOTHER NATURE ABOUND IN THE AREA.

PHOTOS BY PHILIP BEAURLINE

"**P**eople are our most valuable asset. We hire people who like people. It almost sounds phony at times but it's true. They're really the ones that determine our success. When they talk to that customer on the phone, whether it is for a claim or some other area, when they hang up the customer says: "What a nice person. That was great service." Only our employees can do that. We let our people know that we really do value them. We have the lowest turnover ratio of anybody in the insurance industry or in financial services. We make sure our employees have good incomes, good benefits, and a good working environment."

Brian K. Carlson
Regional Vice President
State Farm Insurance

VIRGINIA IS EQUESTRIAN COUNTRY AND SOME OF THE FINEST HUNT CLUBS ARE LOCATED IN THE AREA. FOX HUNTING, POLO MATCHES, AND HORSE SHOWS ARE HELD THROUGHOUT THE REGION. THE MOST POPULAR EQUESTRIAN EVENTS ARE THE FOXFIELD RACES, HELD IN ALBEMARLE COUNTY, AND THE MONTPELIER RACES THAT TAKE PLACE ON THE GROUNDS OF MONTPELIER, HOME OF JAMES MADISON IN ORANGE COUNTY. *PHOTO BY PHILIP BEAURLINE*

A FAVORITE PASTIME IN CHARLOTTESVILLE IS PLAYING A LEISURELY ROUND OF GOLF. AND WITH THE WIDE SELECTION OF FIRST-CLASS GOLF COURSES IT'S EASY TO SEE WHY. AMONG THESE ARE THE SCENIC 500-ACRE BIRDWOOD COURSE (PICTURED ABOVE) AND KESWICK HALL AT MONTICELLO, WHICH OFFERS THE FINEST IN GOLF COURSES, LUXURY RESORTS, AND MEETING FACILITIES. IN 1997, *GOLF DIGEST* RATED CHARLOTTESVILLE AS THE #1 BEST GOLF COMMUNITY FOR RETIREES. *PHOTO BY PHILIP BEAURLINE*

THE CHARLOTTESVILLE AREA CONTAINS HOMES AND NEIGHBOR-
HOODS FOR EVERY TASTE, STYLE, AND INCOME, FROM
ULTRA-MODERN AND SUBURBAN TO ANTIQUE AND URBAN
AND EVERYTHING IN BETWEEN. *PHOTOS BY PHILIP BEAURLINE*

FOR A REGION OF ITS SIZE, THE NUMBER AND VARIETY OF ARTS EVENTS, PERFORMANCES, FESTIVALS, AND EXHIBITIONS IN THE CHARLOTTESVILLE REGION IS IMPRESSIVE. THIS IS A COMMUNITY THAT PROVIDES AN ENTHUSIASTIC AUDIENCE FOR ALMOST EVERY ARTISTIC ENDEAVOR OPEN TO THE PUBLIC. FROM "FRIDAYS AFTER FIVE", WHERE LOCAL BANDS PLAY TO AUDIENCES DURING WARM-WEATHER MONTHS; TO FIRST NIGHT VIRGINIA, WHERE CHARLOTTESVILLE FAMILIES WELCOME THE NEW YEAR IN A SAFE AND FUN-FILLED ENVIRONMENT; TO EVERY HISTORIC PROGRAM AND HOLIDAY EVENT DURING THE YEAR, THE DOWNTOWN MALL EPITOMIZES THE SPIRIT OF THE CHARLOTTESVILLE COMMUNITY.
PHOTOS BY PHILIP BEAURLINE

A PEACH ORCHARD BLOSSOMS, BLANKETING THE HILLSIDE WITH A GLEAMING DISPLAY OF PINK PETALS. *PHOTO BY PHILIP BEAURLINE*

COUNTRY ROADS AND RURAL PASTURES ARE AS COMMON AS COFFEEHOUSES, DINING ESTABLISHMENTS, CINEMAS, AND SHOPPING IN THE CHARLOTTESVILLE REGION, MAKING IT ONE OF THE LIVEABLE CITIES IN THE WORLD. *PHOTOS BY PHILIP BEAURLINE*

ASH LAWN-HIGHLAND, HOME OF PRESIDENT JAMES MONROE, IS ALSO HOME TO MANY CULTURAL EVENTS, INCLUDING CHAMPAGNE AND CANDLELIGHT, KITE DAY, PLANTATION DAYS WEEKEND, AND YULETIDE FESTIVITIES. PERHAPS THE MOST FAMOUS IS THE SUMMER OPERA FESTIVAL, WHICH ALLOWS VISITORS AND LOCALS ALIKE TO ENJOY OPERAS, MUSICAL THEATER PRODUCTIONS, CONCERTS, AND LECTURES THROUGHOUT THE SUMMER MONTHS. *PHOTO BY PHILIP BEAURLINE*

For those who have time to linger at Monticello, specialized guided tours of the gardens and grounds and of the plantation community are available daily during spring, summer, and fall. These tours give visitors a more in-depth glimpse into Jefferson's passion for gardening and a greater understanding of what it took to maintain Monticello's 5,000-acre plantation. The gardens and orchards have been restored to their appearance during Jefferson's lifetime, and many of the trees, vegetables, and flowers that Jefferson cultivated continue to be grown today. A Garden Shop, located near the shuttle station, offers historic plants and seeds grown at Monticello's Thomas Jefferson Center for Historic Plants.

Visitors to Monticello also can walk down "Mulberry Row," where both slave and free workers lived and labored. Named by Jefferson after the trees that lined it, Mulberry Row was the center of plantation activity at Monticello for more than 50 years.

As it was during Jefferson's time, Monticello is still a work-in-progress. The Thomas Jefferson Foundation, which owns and operates Monticello, is undertaking an ambitious project to build the Monticello Gateway and Jefferson History Center. The 95,000 square-foot-complex, to be located on property opposite the current Visitors Center, will include a theater, restaurant, museum, retail shops and guest-service facilities.

A recent addition on the grounds of the Kenwood estate adjacent to Monticello is the Jefferson Library, a 15,500-square-foot, technologically sophisticated facility. Kenwood is the home of Monticello's International Center for Jefferson Studies. Created in 1994 in cooperation with the University of Virginia, the Center grants fellowships to scholars from all over the world, organizes on-site and international conferences, publishes books, and is currently working on the publication of *The Papers of Thomas Jefferson: Retirement Series*. Kenwood is also home to *The Getting Word Oral History Project* that has been locating and recording the oral histories of the descendants of Monticello's enslaved African-American community since 1993.

Located on the Thomas Jefferson Parkway (Route 53), about two miles southeast of Charlottesville, Monticello is open to the public every day except Christmas Day.

Ash Lawn-Highland

Jefferson sought to form an elite community of like-minded souls and encouraged friends like James Madison and James Monroe to settle in Albemarle County. Although Madison preferred to remain at Montpelier, James Monroe did in fact purchase property adjacent to Monticello in 1793, which he named Highland. However, before he could move, Monroe was appointed minister to France. Knowing he would be gone for quite sometime, Monroe entrusted Jefferson with authority to construct a house and plant the orchards at Highland in his absence. The Monroes moved to Highland in November 1799 and considered it their primary residence until 1823.

ALTHOUGH JEFFERSON WAS UNSUCCESSFUL IN LURING JAMES MADISON TO ALBEMARLE COUNTY, MADISON'S ESTATE IN ORANGE WAS JUST A DAY'S CARRIAGE RIDE AWAY. LOCATED IN THE FOOTHILLS OF THE BLUE RIDGE MOUNTAINS, MADISON DESCRIBED MONTPELIER AS "A SQUIRREL'S JUMP FROM HEAVEN." *PHOTO BY PHILIP BEAURLINE*

Monroe intended Highland to be a working farm and, like Jefferson, experimented with diverse crops and planting methods while continually making improvements to the property in anticipation of his retirement. Unfortunately, pressing debts forced Monroe to sell Highland in 1826, the same year Jefferson died. Alexander Garrett purchased the property in 1837 and sometime during his ownership the estate's name changed to Ash Lawn. In the 1880s, John Massey, a retired Baptist minister and later Lieutenant Governor of Virginia, built the two-story Victorian section of the house, expanding the house to its present size. The Massey family owned Ash Lawn until 1930 when Jay Winston Johns purchased the plantation. In 1974 he willed the property to Monroe and Jefferson's alma mater, the College of William and Mary, "for the education of the general public."

Each year, close to 100,000 visitors drive up Ash Lawn-Highland's expansive, ash tree lined driveway to partake in the beauty of this remarkable 535-acre estate. Guests get a taste of what a working plantation was like with demonstrations of such things as tin-smithing and open-hearth cooking. Children have fun visiting the sheep and rolling hoops on the lawn and enjoy a picnic lunch with their parents.

ESTABLISHED IN 1784 BY SCOTSMAN WILLIAM MICHIE, MICHIE TAVERN TODAY ALLOWS VISITORS A STEP BACK IN TIME. FROM ITS PERIOD-CLAD HOST TO HEARTY SOUTHERN DISHES, THE TAVERN IS A PLACE TO LEAVE THIS CENTURY AND ENTER A TIME GONE BY. BUT IT'S NOT JUST A PLACE TO DINE; MICHIE TAVERN HAS A LOT TO EXPERIENCE--DEPENDANT OUTBUILDINGS, THE VIRGINIA WINE MUSEUM, THE SOWELL HOUSE, AND THE MEADOW RUN GRIST MILL. *PHOTO BY PHILIP BEAURLINE*

Ash Lawn-Highland is renowned for its century-old exquisite boxwood gardens. The English and American boxwoods emit an intoxicating aroma that has become synonymous with Monroe's former estate. Inside Monroe's home, visitors are treated to a variety of furnishings and decorative items from both the eighteenth and nineteenth centuries. Although Monroe's home was typical of farmhouses in the 1800s, its elegant French, English and American crafted furnishings make this house anything but typical today. With an historic precedent set by the Monroe's daughter Eliza, who was wed at Highland, the property continues to be a storybook locale for small, intimate outdoor weddings in the spring and fall months.

Ash Lawn-Highland has an ambitious agenda of special events planned throughout the year. Most famous of these is the Summer Festival that began more than 20 years ago as an extension of Ash Lawn-Highland's interpretive program to illustrate the cultural life of the Monroe Era. Recognized by *Money* Magazine as one of the international top-20 warm weather summer opera companies, the Summer Festival also presents Music at Twilight (a potpourri of classical, jazz, folk, and contemporary music), Summer Saturdays (music, dance, and puppetry for the entire family), and Plantation Days at Highland (period craft demonstrations and living history reenactments).

Ash Lawn-Highland, located at 1000 James Monroe Parkway just 2-1/2 miles from Monticello, is open daily except for New Year's Day, Thanksgiving Day, and Christmas Day.

Michie Tavern ca. 1784

Michie Tavern is one of the few historic properties in the Charlottesville area where visitors experience eighteenth century hospitality first-hand. Established in 1784 by Scotsman William Michie, the Tavern was frequented by travelers who stopped for food, drink, and lodging. Much like those eighteenth century travelers, people who visit the Tavern today are greeted by a host dressed in period attire. The Michie Tavern is known for its authentic hearty midday fare consisting of recipes dating back to the 1700s. The Tavern's dining rooms, the Ordinary, feature a southern buffet of succulent Colonial Fried Chicken, a variety of hot and cold dishes, and a delicious apple cobbler dessert. During the colder months, hot green beans, homemade mashed potatoes and gravy, and homemade garden vegetable soup help take the edge off a crisp Virginia day. Throughout the year a variety of beverages, including Virginia wines, hot or cold cider, and traditional lagers are available.

After the meal, visitors may tour Mr. Michie's Tavern, which earned its landmark status for its role in the 1920s preservation movement when the original inn was relocated seventeen miles to its current location near Monticello. The tour recreates eighteenth century tavern history through a lively, hands-on living history program. Afterwards, guests tour the Tavern's dependent outbuildings, the Virginia Wine Museum, and the Meadow Run Grist Mill. The Printer's Market, General Store, and Museum Gift Shop offer a variety of quality gifts, including historic originals, historic representations, and collectibles. Michie Tavern is open seven days a week, year-round. Located on the Thomas Jefferson Parkway, it is Monticello's closest historic neighbor.

The Presidents Pass, a combination discount ticket for touring Monticello, Ash Lawn-Highland, and Michie Tavern is available at the Charlottesville/Albemarle Convention & Visitors Bureau located on Route 20 South in the Monticello Visitor Center building.

Montpelier

Although Jefferson was unsuccessful in luring James Madison to Albemarle County, Madison's estate in Orange was just a day's carriage ride away. Located in the foothills of the Blue Ridge Mountains, Madison described Montpelier as "a squirrel's jump from heaven" and after exploring this magnificent plantation, visitors soon reach the same conclusion.

Montpelier was home to three generations of Madisons, beginning in 1723 when James Madison's grandfather was first deeded the land until 1844 when Dolley Madison sold the estate. Montpelier changed ownership six times before William and Annie duPont purchased the estate in 1900 and expanded the house. Their daughter, Marion duPont Scott, built two racecourses and started the Montpelier Hunt Races-an annual equestrian celebration. Mrs. Scott bequeathed the

HOME TO OUR NATION'S FOURTH PRESIDENT, JAMES MADISON, MONTPELIER IS RICH IN HISTORY. ARCHEOLOGICAL DIGS ARE PROVIDING MORE INFORMATION ABOUT THIS EXCITING ESTATE. THESE INVESTIGATIONS HAVE DISCOVERED A NUMBER OF ARTIFACTS THAT REVEAL MORE ABOUT DAILY ACTIVITIES AT MONTPELIER, INCLUDING JEWELRY, STRAIGHT PINS, THIMBLES, AND SMOKING PIPES. *PHOTOS BY PHILIP BEAURLINE*

property to the National Trust for Historic Preservation in 1983. Compared to Monticello and Ash Lawn, Montpelier is a young historic property and is just in the beginning stages of its development as a memorial to our fourth president's contributions and ideals.

Visitors to Montpelier have much to see. A 15-minute orientation video about the Madisons, shown in the Mansion, starts off each visit. An Acoustiguide audio tour system enables visitors to explore the house at their own pace. Highlights in the home include the dining room-a re-creation of the room where Dolley and James Madison entertained visitors from around the world-and the growing collection of Madison furnishings and artifacts that are coming home to Montpelier.

The spacious grounds also hold treasures for visitors-the Garden Temple, built by Madison to cover a 24-foot ice well; the Back Lawn, where Dolley held her famous barbecues; the terraced, two-acre formal Garden; the Madison family and slave cemeteries; active archaeological sites, where Montpelier staff and volunteers unearth the history of Montpelier; and breathtaking vistas of the Blue Ridge Mountains. Also worth exploring is the James Madison Landmark Forest, a 200-acre old-growth forest with trees from Madison's lifetime.

Located four miles south of Orange on Route 20 (the Constitution Highway), Montpelier is open daily except for New Year's Day, Thanksgiving, Christmas Eve, and Christmas.

The University of Virginia

From a strictly historical perspective, Thomas Jefferson's Academical Village is the encapsulation of the American dream. Designed to allow students and faculty to live and work side by side, the University of Virginia has been a model to educational institutions around the world. Proclaimed the most significant architectural achievement of the nation's first 200 years by the American Institute of Architects, the University is one of 400 sites around the world named to the World Heritage List in recognition of its universal cultural value. Jefferson devoted the latter part of his life to the design and construction of the University and considered it one of his crowning achievements.

Jefferson's Academical Village was built around The Lawn, a rectangular grassy area that is the heart and soul of the University. At the end of the Lawn is The Rotunda, an impressive building that serves as the landmark by which most people identify the University. Most visits begin at the Rotunda, the University's original library and classroom building, which can be explored alone or with a student guide. Built between 1823 and 1826 and designed as a half-scale interpretation of the Pantheon in Rome, the Rotunda was destroyed in a fire in October 1895 and rebuilt with some alterations to Jefferson's original plan. In anticipation of the country's bicentennial, the Rotunda was restored to Jefferson's design in 1973. The Rotunda's oval rooms and the Dome Room are used for meetings, dinners, special ceremonies, and student activities.

The Lawn is flanked by two rows of identical, one-story rooms reserved for outstanding student leaders in their final year of study. Despite the rooms' cramped 15-square-foot size and lack of indoor plumbing, students consider it a privilege to reside here. The student rooms are accentuated by 10 large Pavilions that appear much as they did in the 1820s. Jefferson designed the Pavilions so no two would look alike—each facade is reflective of the architecture of ancient Rome, which was influenced by Jefferson's study of Andrea Palladio's *Four Books of Architecture* as well as his extensive travels throughout Europe. Senior faculty members and their families live in nine of the Pavilions with classes meeting regularly in two. Pavilion VII, the University's first building, is home to the Colonnade Club, a faculty organization.

Behind the Pavilions are the public gardens that were restored by the Garden Club of Virginia. Little is known about the original gardens, but engravings from the 1820s of the University's overall plan show the locations of the famous one-brick-thick serpentine walls that visitors continue to admire today.

THE UNIVERSITY OF VIRGINIA IS ONE OF 400 SITES AROUND THE WORLD NAMED TO THE WORLD HERITAGE LIST IN RECOGNITION OF ITS UNIVERSAL CULTURAL VALUE. THOMAS JEFFERSON DEVOTED THE LATTER PART OF HIS LIFE TO THE DESIGN AND CONSTRUCTION OF THE UNIVERSITY. *PHOTO BY PHILIP BEAURLINE*

Other Historic Sites

A good way to get an overview of the many historic sites throughout the Charlottesville area is to visit the Albemarle County Historical Society in downtown Charlottesville. The Society offers a number of exhibits, tours, publications, and other programs to promote an awareness and appreciation for the area's history. From April through October, the Society gives walking tours of historic downtown Charlottesville every Saturday at 10:00 am. During the one-hour tour, visitors stroll around historic Court Square, an area that was so familiar to Jefferson, Madison, and Monroe.

For Civil War buffs, there are numerous Confederate sites through the Charlottesville/Albemarle area, including Orange County's Wilderness Civil War Battlefield.

And while Monticello, Montpelier, and Ash Lawn-Highland are among the most famous historic homes in the region, visitors have also enjoyed side trips to the Barboursville Ruins; the Hoover Camp, President Herbert Hoover's "Summer White House" in Madison County; the Madison-Barbour Historic District in Orange County which is the largest rural historic district in Virginia; and the Oak Ridge Estate, a 5,000-acre plantation built in 1802, in Nelson County, to name a few.

With an area as rich in history as the Charlottesville Region, it would take an entire book to do justice to a fraction of all of the homes, estates, churches, and sites that are open to the public. From the early eighteenth century settlements, through the Revolutionary and Civil Wars, right up to the present, the historic legacy of this area is a treasure that continues to be honored and preserved for future generations. ■

THE CITY OF CHARLOTTESVILLE AND THE SURROUNDING AREAS ARE STEEPED IN AMERICAN HISTORY. HOME TO MANY OF OUR COUNTRY'S FOUNDING FATHERS, CHARLOTTESVILLE GRACEFULLY TAKES ITS RESIDENTS AND VISITORS BACK IN TIME WITH MUSEUMS, HOMES AND PLANTATIONS, CHURCHES, AND CEMETERIES. *PHOTOS BY PHILIP BEAURLINE*

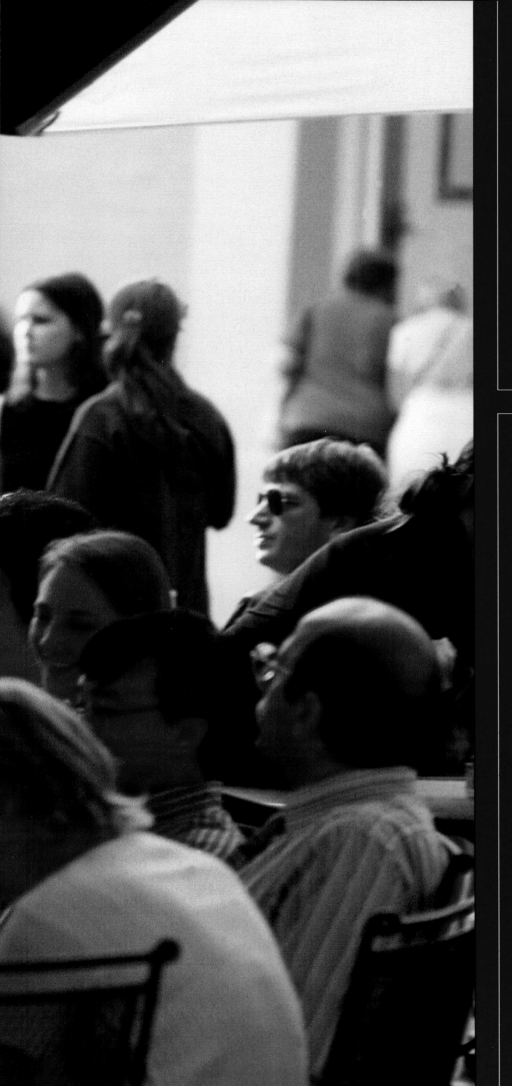

CHAPTER THREE

A STRONG, DIVERSIFIED ECONOMY

......

"Agriculture, manufactures, commerce, and navigation, the four pillars of our prosperity, are the most thriving when left most free to individual enterprise."

— Thomas Jefferson
First Annual Presidential Message, 1801

THE CITY OF CHARLOTTESVILLE HAS ENJOYED A RENAISSANCE IN RECENT YEARS WITH THE REVITALIZATION OF THE DOWNTOWN AREA AND THE WEST MAIN STREET CORRIDOR THAT SERVES AS A LINK TO THE UNIVERSITY OF VIRGINIA. THE STEADY, STABLE LOCAL ECONOMY IS SOMEWHAT OF AN ANOMALY IN THAT IT DOES NOT DEPEND ON A TRADITIONAL LARGE EMPLOYER BASE, BUT RATHER ON AN UNUSUALLY HIGH SMALL BUSINESS SECTOR. *PHOTO BY PHILIP BEAURLINE*

The Charlottesville region enjoys a highly diversified economy comprised of a strong commercial and service sector, light manufacturing, education, and health services anchored by the University of Virginia and a thriving heritage tourism trade. With a per capita income of close to $31,000 (Charlottesville & Albemarle County, 1998), the region has an increasing number of quality jobs and a strong labor pool that pulls from a population base of more than 210,000 people living in the City of Charlottesville and surrounding seven counties. As a result, the area has an unemployment rate that is consistently much lower than the state and national averages.

Charlottesville serves as the commercial and market center for a multi-county trade area in central Virginia. One of the reasons that businesses find the region so appealing is its close proximity to Richmond and Washington, D.C. People who have grown weary of big city congestion and long commutes find the

Charlottesville area a viable alternative. A convenient transportation system consisting of a safe, efficient major interstate and highway system, a modern airport, and Amtrak help link the area to worldwide destinations.

The region's steady, stable economy is somewhat of an anomaly in that it does not depend on a traditional large employer base, but rather on an unusually high number of small and emerging businesses. This factor, coupled with the presence of the University and a thriving tourist trade, has made the area less susceptible to recession and the "boom-to-bust" economic swings that plague other communities. Safeguarding the region's small business status is of primary concern to area residents. Ever vigilant over maintaining the inseparable link between a vibrant economy and quality of life, the Charlottesville Regional Chamber of Commerce works with area governments to maintain this essential connection.

The City of Charlottesville has enjoyed a renaissance in recent years with the revitalization of its historic

NOTHING COMPLEMENTS A CRISP, VIRGINIA DAY BETTER THAN A GLASS OF WINE FROM ONE OF THE COUNTRY'S BEST WINERIES. THE CHARLOTTESVILLE AREA IS RENOWNED FOR ITS FIRST-CLASS WINERIES AND VINEYARDS. WITH THEIR QUAINT FARMS, SPRAWLING LANDSCAPE, AND BREATHTAKING VIEWS OF THE BLUE RIDGE MOUNTAINS, THE VINEYARDS OF VIRGINIA ARE MAGNIFICENT. MOST OFFER TASTINGS OF VARIOUS WINES SURE TO PLEASE ANY PALATE. *PHOTO BY PHILIP BEAURLINE*

SHOPS OF ALL KINDS CAN BE FOUND IN CHARLOTTESVILLE. THE
CITY HAS EVERYTHING FROM HISTORIC MOM AND POP STORES
TO MODERN MALLS TO MAKE FINDING THAT SOMETHING SPECIAL
EASY AND CONVENIENT. *PHOTO BY PHILIP BEAURLINE*

Whether coming to partake in the beauty of the area, to enjoy its many cultural and historic sites, or to transact business, visitors contribute a significant income to the area's many hotels, restaurants, and specialty shops. In 1997, Charlottesville was ranked among the top 10 of the Most Visited City and Most Favorite Meeting Destination in Virginia. Of the 40 cities and 95 counties in Virginia, Charlottesville and Albemarle County rank tenth and ninth respectively in total travel revenue. More than 21,000 local residents either directly or indirectly rely on the travel industry for their livelihood. Tax revenues from sales, real estate, meal, income, and accommodation taxes generated by visitors in Charlottesville and Albemarle County in 1998 equaled $8,580,000, an increase of more than 12 percent from the previous year.

Of all the factors contributing to the economic growth of the area, the University of Virginia is the single largest economic engine in the community. As the largest public employer in the area with some 12,000

downtown area and the West Main Street corridor that serves as a link to the University of Virginia. Because the availability of city land is a premium, emphasis has been placed on economic redevelopment, with properties along the city's commercial corridors being renovated at a record pace. Charlottesville's bend toward mixed development—with residential, business, and retail centers being combined in a single building—has transformed the downtown area from a 9 to 5 work center to a vibrant 24-hour community.

One of the fastest growing segments of business development within the City of Charlottesville is the high-technology industry. Recognizing that emerging technology businesses bring with them an upwardly mobile educated workforce to fill cutting-edge jobs, the city has been designated as a "technology zone" with low business licensing fees designed to entice companies to locate within the city. This has not been a hard sell, as the ambiance of the restaurants, shopping, and entertainment found downtown has made it the location of choice for a number of technology businesses.

A major contributor to the area's economy traditionally has been the travel and tourism trade. Charlottesville and Albemarle County's share of travel and tourism dollars was more than $253 million in 1998 and growing. In an area rich in history, visitors from all over the world continue to flock to Monticello, the University of Virginia, and other historic points of interest each year. Local vineyards, which have gained a national reputation with their fine Virginia wines, attract numerous visitors each year, as do the breathtaking Blue Ridge Parkway and Wintergreen, the area's year-round mountain resort.

FROM QUAINT COFFEEHOUSES TO GOURMET RESTAURANTS,
THERE IS SOMETHING FOR EVERY TASTE IN CHARLOTTESVILLE.
CHARLOTTESVILLE OFFERS CASUAL INNS SERVING OLD-FASHIONED
SOUTHERN FARE, HISTORIC TAVERNS WITH A FEEL FOR DAYS GONE
BY, AND ELEGANT RESTAURANTS SERVING THE FINEST GOURMET
MEALS. ETHNIC RESTAURANTS RANGING FROM MEXICAN TO THAI,
ITALIAN TO MIDDLE EASTERN ALSO PROVIDE THE AREA WITH A
MYRIAD OF CHOICES. *PHOTO BY PHILIP BEAURLINE*

NEW CONSTRUCTION, THE HALLMARK OF A HEALTHY ECONOMY, CAN BE SEEN IN BOTH THE REGION'S RESIDENTIAL AND COMMERCIAL SECTORS. ON THE OUTSKIRTS OF TOWN, HOMES ARE BEING BUILT IN NEW SUBDIVISIONS TO KEEP PACE WITH THE INFLUX OF NEW RESIDENTS. NEW BUSINESS PARKS ARE PART OF THE PLAN TO DRAW MORE TECHNOLOGY COMPANIES TO THE AREA. COMBINING NATURE AND TECHNOLOGY, THE NORTH FORK RESEARCH PARK EXPANDS 562 SPRAWLING ACRES AND INCLUDES SPACE FOR EVERYTHING FROM OFFICE BUILDINGS TO MEDICAL AND RESEARCH LABORATORIES ALL CRADLED BY THE BREATHTAKING LANDSCAPE OF VIRGINIA. *PHOTOS BY PHILIP BEAURLINE*

retirees chose the Charlottesville region primarily to golf and relax. While the amenities of the region continue to attract mature residents, many are choosing Charlottesville because it is ripe for new business development. After researching the area, many young-at-heart entrepreneurs find the Charlottesville region ideal for starting second careers and invest their money into developing new businesses that add to the wealth and value of the community at large.

As with other segments of life in the Charlottesville region, when it comes to the economy the biggest challenge continues to be maintaining a steady, stable growth compatible with the natural aesthetics of the area. Because growth and development are done on a regional basis, addressing these concerns means bringing people together on a multi-jurisdictional basis and taking a balanced approach to growth, transportation, and maintaining the quality of life.

To that end, the Charlottesville area has the opportunity to become world-class in terms of demonstrating how economic growth and those attributes that define quality of life can be maintained in perpetuity. Up until now, growth has been successfully targeted in selected areas. The quality of life of the area has been sustained. ■

workers-about half of whom work for the University's nationally ranked Medical Center-the University has been credited with driving the area's economic growth. It is said, as the University goes, so goes the community. In times of significant growth, there is generally a link to a corresponding event taking place at the University. This was especially apparent in the 1970s when the University expanded its scope by admitting undergraduate women. Throughout its history, the University has brought in people from all over the world, creating a cosmopolitan community of students, teachers, and researchers, many of whom choose to remain in the community and add to the area's economic prosperity. Today, the University focuses on building new research parks and developing mutually beneficial partnerships with the local business community to attract more bio-tech and info-tech companies with higher paying jobs that will inevitably boost the economy even further.

Moving outside of Charlottesville and Albemarle County, the adjacent rural counties are seeing an unprecedented economic boom as well. Fluvanna County to the east is the second fastest growing county in Virginia; Greene County to the north is sixth. With lower housing costs and greater availability of land, these areas are experiencing an influx of people who want the advantages of living in a more rural community yet being within a short drive of work, culture, entertainment, and health care services.

Just as the technology companies are attracting a youthful affluence to the area, an equally viable mature population is also thriving. In the past,

CHARLOTTESVILLE SERVES AS THE COMMERCIAL AND MARKET CENTER FOR A MULTI-COUNTY TRADE AREA IN CENTRAL VIRGINIA.
ONE OF THE REASONS THAT BUSINESSES FIND THE REGION SO APPEALING IS ITS CLOSE PROXIMITY TO RICHMOND AND WASHINGTON, D.C.
PHOTO BY PHILIP BEAURLINE

LEFT: THOSE COMING TO VISIT THE CHARLOTTESVILLE AREA FOR BUSINESS OR JUST A RELAXING VACATION WILL FIND THAT GETTING THERE IS
HALF THE FUN WITH THE CHARLOTTESVILLE/ALBEMARLE AIRPORT. THIS MODERN FACILITY, WHICH OFFERS FLIGHT SCHOOLS AND AIRCRAFT
CHARTER FIRMS, NOT ONLY LINKS CHARLOTTESVILLE WITH THE REST OF THE WORLD, BUT ALSO IS A STAPLE IN THE GROWING ECONOMY
OF THE AREA. RIGHT: WHILE THE RICH HISTORY OF CHARLOTTESVILLE MAY TAKE YOU BACK IN TIME; THE GROWING ECONOMY HAS THRUST
THE CITY INTO THE TWENTY-FIRST CENTURY. A STATE-OF-THE-ART RAIL SYSTEM ONLY ADDS TO THIS GROWTH BY PROVIDING A SAFE AND
ECONOMICAL WAY TO TRAVEL, AND WITH SEVERAL TRIPS LEAVING DAILY, A CONVENIENT ONE, TOO. *PHOTOS BY PHILIP BEAURLINE*

IN CHARLOTTESVILLE, THE BRIGHTEST MINDS IN BUSINESS HAVE A PLACE TO COME AND CONDUCT RESEARCH, EXCHANGE IDEAS, AND INTERACT WITH THE UNIVERSITY AND COMMUNITY. THE STRENGTHS OF THE PAST ARE INTERTWINED WITH THE VISION OF TOMORROW TO CREATE ONE OF THE MOST EXTRAORDINARY BUSINESS ENVIRONMENTS IN NORTH AMERICA. *PHOTOS BY PHILIP BEAURLINE*

"**S**print's Charlottesville-Albemarle County area presence is significant in terms of employees and services offered, and in terms of providing volunteers and contributions to our communities. On the operations side, Sprint is a complete, integrated, solutions provider, offering services and products to meet the needs of even the most demanding business customer. We have invested millions of dollars in network infrastructure in facilities and in economic development efforts. Charlottesville was the first community in the nation to receive Sprint's FastConnect DSL service, and the local footprint continues to expand, as does the company's desire to be the communications provider of choice for the region."

Margaret Wright
Regional Public Affairs Manager
Sprint

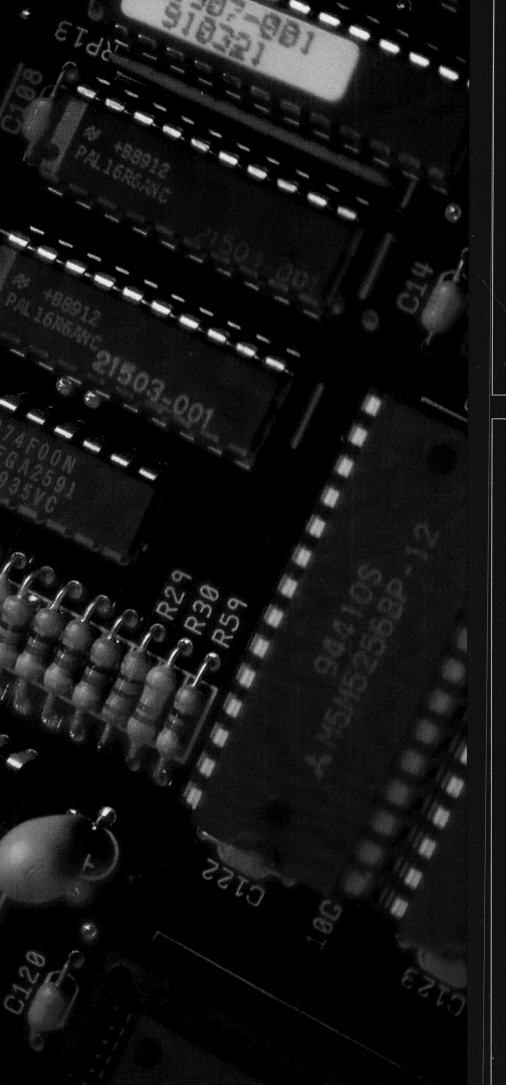

4 | CHAPTER FOUR

A CRADLE FOR HIGH-TECH VISIONARIES

· · · · · ·

"Where a new invention is supported by well known principles, and promises to be useful, it ought to be tried."

— Thomas Jefferson
Letter to Robert Fulton, 1810

LURED TO THE AREA BECAUSE OF ITS VITAL
ECONOMY, EDUCATED WORKFORCE, PHYSICAL
BEAUTY, QUALITY OF LIFE, AND THE RESOURCES
OF THE UNIVERSITY OF VIRGINIA, THE INFLUX
OF NEW AND RELOCATING TECHNOLOGY
COMPANIES HAS POSITIVELY IMPACTED
THE COMMUNITY CHARACTER.
PHOTO © ERIC BERNDT

Looking at the burgeoning list of technology businesses that now call the Charlottesville region home, it is hard to imagine that only a few years ago technology companies in Central Virginia were very few. Although Charlottesville has long been home to several large employers who were involved in technology—such as GE Fanuc and Litton Marine, Inc.—the growth in emerging technology companies began to accelerate only in the late 1990s.

Lured to the area because of its vital economy, educated workforce, physical beauty, quality of life, and the resources of the University of Virginia, the influx of new and relocating technology companies has positively impacted the community character. A stroll on the Downtown Mall or a respite at a local coffeehouse gives visitors a glimpse at the growing youthful zest and affluence that is revitalizing the downtown area with an economic shot-in-the-arm.

The presence of the University of Virginia has been a significant factor in growing and enticing technology companies to the Charlottesville area. Millions of dollars

in research funds pour into the University each year, the vast majority of which are dedicated to medical research. Fueled by this huge investment, companies producing medical devices, pharmaceuticals, and other types of health care innovations have a tremendous opportunity to grow in the Charlottesville region.

The University also has implemented policies to encourage high technology growth in the area. University of Virginia Gateway, for example, was created as an outreach effort of the University's Vice President for Research and Public Service to represent the University's interests in the development of Central Virginia's high technology business sector. Gateway promotes beneficial relationships between high-tech companies and the University's research efforts; it assists University faculty members in developing start-up companies to commercialize on their research; it acts as the University's representative in public/private partnerships dedicated to technology business growth; and it serves as a public service representative of the University in day-to-day contacts with public officials, private business leaders, and the public.

Organizations like Gateway are one reason that Charlottesville is so attractive to high-tech companies. A unified vision is another. The region fosters an enthusiastic spirit of cooperation among private enterprise, state and local government officials, schools, and the community at large in supporting technology initiatives that make owning, operating, or working for a technology business in Charlottesville such a positive experience. This cooperative movement has spawned numerous organizations that provide continuing education through classes, programs, and networking opportunities.

One of the fastest growing and most active groups in the area is The Virginia Piedmont Technology Council (VPTC). A membership organization representing technology companies, VPTC provides a forum for advocating technology development among the government, public, and private sectors. It hosts a monthly luncheon series featuring guest speakers and providing time for business leaders to network with each other. VPTC offers programs, services, and encouragement in the areas of education, capital formation, business networking, workforce development, legislative affairs, communications, and regional implementation of technology.

VPTC is one of several high-tech organizations that share offices, classrooms, and meeting space at The Connected Community Technology Center. Located in an 11,500 square foot former industrial warehouse, the Connected Community is an innovative public/private partnership between VPTC, the City of Charlottesville, Albemarle County, Piedmont Virginia Community College, Virginia's Center for Innovative Technology, the University of Virginia, the Orange County School System, and a number of businesses.

AS NEW TECHNOLOGY BUSINESSES GROW OR MOVE INTO THE AREA, UNIVERSITY OF VIRGINIA GRADUATES ARE BECOMING AN INCREASING SOURCE FOR FILLING THE AVAILABLE HIGH-TECH POSITIONS. *PHOTO © MICHAEL RUSH*

THE UNIVERSITY OF VIRGINIA RESEARCH PARK AT NORTH FORK SITS ON 562 ACRES AND CONTAINS THREE MILLION SQUARE FEET OF SPACE ZONED FOR OFFICES, LIGHT INDUSTRY, A HOTEL AND CONFERENCE CENTER, LABORATORY, MEDICAL, AND PHARMACEUTICAL RESEARCH AND DEVELOPMENT, AND RETAIL USES AS WELL. *PHOTO BY PHILIP BEAURLINE*

In addition to VPTC, the Center is home to Computers4Kids, a non-profit organization that provides refurbished computers to children who do not have computers at home. Piedmont Virginia Community College (PVCC) has set up several computer learning laboratories and its Biotechnology Center at the Connected Community Center, which also serves as headquarters for the Information Technology (I.T.) Academy, and for a prototype robotics manufacturing facility. With so many high-tech venues under one roof, the Center works toward bridging the digital divide by providing a site where everyone can learn about and use new technologies.

The Neon Guild is another technology-oriented association. Comprised of Internet professionals in the area, the Guild provides a casual and friendly atmosphere for tech people to form relationships, ask questions, promote services, find a job, or hire an employee. Many Guild members share their time and talent in mentoring high school students, teaching, and donating their equipment-all in the spirit of helping others in the community explore the high-tech field.

As new technology businesses grow or move into the area, University graduates are becoming an increasing source for filling the available high-tech positions.

That was not always the case. In the past, University graduates who may have wanted to remain in the area were unable to do so because the jobs they were looking for could only be found in larger cities. That is starting to change. Nonetheless, with a national shortage of information technology personnel, a number of innovative educational programs designed to create a more regional technology workforce have been implemented throughout the Charlottesville area public school systems.

One example of building this workforce is PVCC's Center for Training and Workforce Development, a state-of-the-art training and development service offering custom computer training to businesses, industry, and government. The Center has an ongoing program of computer training courses and two non-credit certificate programs: Professional Design and Business Computing Applications. The Professional Design program has two components from which to choose: Web Design Fundamentals, which offers instruction in Web design principles and theory; and MultiMedia Design that trains individuals in multimedia design and production.

A major contributor in workforce training and development is The Charlottesville Area Business and School Alliance (CASBA), also housed in The Connected

Community Technology Center. Founded in 1996 by local businesses seeking better ways of working with public schools, CASBA provides a variety of opportunities for students and teachers to interact with technology companies through job fairs, internships, job shadowing, and mentorships.

In order to further develop the local technology workforce, a "virtual" Information Technology Academy was formed to assist area high school students in identifying and defining a high-tech career they're interested in, then pointing them to resources to help them continue along that pathway. To achieve this, the I.T. Academy offers a coordinated series of academic electives, providing online resources, distance learning, workplace experiences, enrichment activities, and technology training courses focused on information technology career pathways. Through the I.T. Academy, students receive the technology skills and knowledge base needed to successfully transition to a four-year college, community college, or employment.

The I.T. Academy is an extension of the philosophy and vision of the Charlottesville Albemarle Technical Education Center (CATEC). Built in 1973, CATEC continues to provide career and technical education to prepare individuals to excel in a career, to further their education, and to enhance their life skills through academic and technical studies that reflect the workforce needs of the community.

With a skilled workforce backed by numerous pro-technology programs all in an area that is at the same time home to a vibrant economy and one of the most desirable places in the country to live, it is not surprising that entrepreneurs and corporations alike overcome obstacles to relocate or start their companies in the Charlottesville area. Growth can challenge a community. While embracing growth, Charlottesville also prizes its small-town appeal. The Charlottesville region continues to build on its strong technology-based economy while enhancing the heritage, beauty, and quality of life that adds to the region's economic vitality. ■

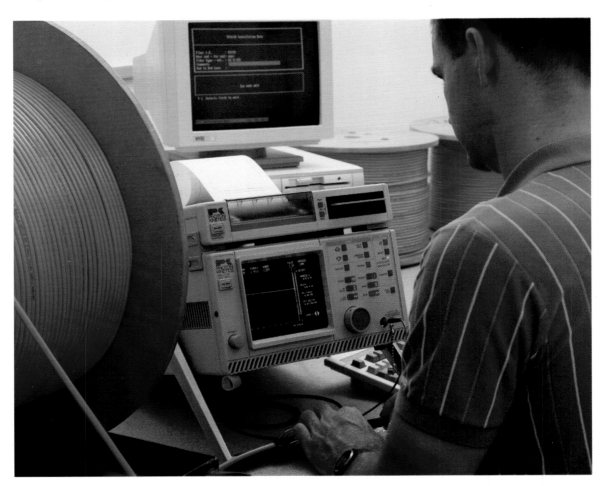

THE CHARLOTTESVILLE REGION FOSTERS AN ENTHUSIASTIC SPIRIT OF COOPERATION AMONG PRIVATE ENTERPRISE, STATE AND LOCAL GOVERNMENT OFFICIALS, SCHOOLS, AND THE COMMUNITY AT LARGE IN SUPPORTING TECHNOLOGY INITIATIVES THAT FACILITATE OWNING, OPERATING, OR WORKING FOR A TECHNOLOGY BUSINESS IN CHARLOTTESVILLE. *PHOTO © JOHN MUTREX*

ABOVE: THE PRESENCE OF THE UNIVERSITY OF VIRGINIA HAS BEEN A SIGNIFICANT FACTOR IN GROWING AND ENTICING TECHNOLOGY COMPANIES TO THE CHARLOTTESVILLE AREA. MILLIONS OF DOLLARS IN RESEARCH FUNDS POUR INTO THE UNIVERSITY EACH YEAR, THE VAST MAJORITY OF WHICH ARE DEDICATED TO MEDICAL RESEARCH. BELOW: COMPANIES PRODUCING MEDICAL DEVICES, PHARMACEUTICALS, AND OTHER TYPES OF HEALTH CARE INNOVATIONS HAVE A TREMENDOUS OPPORTUNITY TO GROW IN THE CHARLOTTESVILLE REGION.
PHOTOS BY PHILIP BEAURLINE

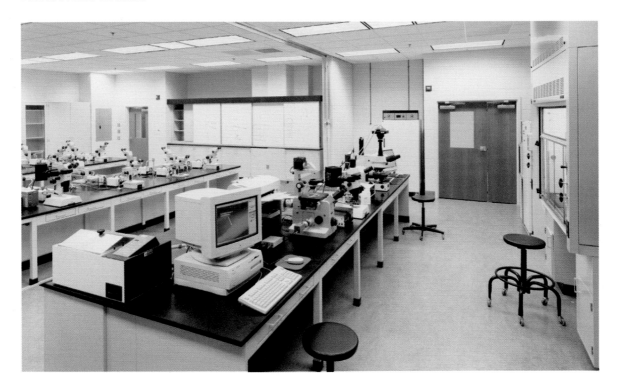

A MECCA FOR THE ARTS

· · · · ·

*"I am an enthusiast on the subject of the arts.
But it is an enthusiasm of which I am not
ashamed, as its object is to improve the taste
of my countrymen, to increase their reputation,
to reconcile them to the respect of the world,
and procure them its praise."*

— *Thomas Jefferson*
Letter to James Madison, 1785

CHARLOTTESVILLE IS A CITY WHERE THE CREATIVE
ARTS ABOUND. WHETHER IT'S FEATURED IN
LOCAL GALLERIES OR HANGING IN RESTAURANTS,
ARTWORK CAN BE FOUND EVERYWHERE. BUT ITS
NOT JUST PAINTINGS THAT ARE ABUNDANT.
MUSIC FESTIVALS, THEATER GROUPS, AUTHOR
READING AND BOOK SIGNINGS, AND PERFORMING
ARTS CENTERS ARE ALL SUPPORTED AND
ENCOURAGED IN CHARLOTTESVILLE. TO KEEP
THIS CREATIVE FIRE GOING, THE UNIVERSITY OF
VIRGINIA, IN ITS VIRGINIA 2020 INITIATIVE, IS
WORKING TO RAISE MILLIONS TO STRENGTHEN
THE CULTURAL ENVIRONMENT OF ITSELF AND
CHARLOTTESVILLE. *PHOTO BY PHILIP BEAURLINE*

If a "Mecca" can be described as the place where one goes to fulfill his or her goals and ambitions, the Charlottesville region is indeed a "Mecca" for the arts. With the cultural life of a large city but the intimacy of a small town, the Charlottesville area has lured artists and patrons alike and has quietly developed into a sophisticated arts savvy community.

Charlottesville's physical beauty has long been an inspiration to artists in all venues. From the breath-taking mountains to the tranquil pastoral countryside, artists from all over the world have created a large and diverse cultural environment in which the creative arts are flourishing.

For a region of its size, the number and variety of arts events, performances, festivals, and exhibitions in the Charlottesville region is impressive. This is a community that provides an enthusiastic audience for almost every artistic endeavor open to the public. The fact that many performances are sold-out is a testament to the region's endorsement of local performing artists. Businesses support new programs, exhibits, and performances. It is not unusual to see paintings of local artists on display in the dining rooms of restaurants or the lobbies of law firms. The community as a whole embraces its artists, doing what it can to help each succeed in a field that is not always kind to its novices.

Home to the famous and the as-yet-undiscovered, artists can be found around every corner in Charlottesville—from galleries downtown to the more isolated studios in remote mountain areas. To accommodate and showcase its talented residents, the Charlottesville region has numerous performing arts centers, music festivals, studios, galleries, museums, theater groups, and support organizations in place to enable artists to showcase their work and network with other artists.

One of the most renowned of all celebrations of the arts is the Ash Lawn-Highland Summer Festival. The beautiful boxwood gardens at the historic home of President James Monroe serve as the backdrop for what

CHARLOTTESVILLE COMBINES ALL THE ELEMENTS OF A WORLD-CLASS CITY-A THRIVING ECONOMY, INNOVATIVE HEALTH CARE, QUALITY SCHOOLS, RICH HISTORY-BUT PERHAPS ITS MOST UNIQUE ELEMENT IS ITS FOCUS ON CULTURE. ARTS AND MUSIC ARE PART OF EVERYDAY LIFE. THE GREAT EMPHASIS PLACED ON THEATER, ARTS, AND MUSIC MAKES CHARLOTTESVILLE A TRULY MAGNIFICENT PLACE TO LIVE, WORK, AND VISIT. *PHOTO BY PHILIP BEAURLINE*

ABOVE: ART IN ALL ITS FORMS AND STYLES HAS A PLACE AND A PURPOSE IN CHARLOTTESVILLE, WHETHER IT'S A WELL-KNOWN WORK EXHIBITED IN ONE OF THE CITY'S MUSEUMS OR GALLERIES OR A PIECE OF SPLASHY POP ART SUCH AS THIS MURAL OUTSIDE THE PARAMOUNT THEATER. BELOW: SITTING QUIETLY AS A STATELY REMINDER OF THE CITY'S PAST, THE PARAMOUNT THEATER REMAINS AN IMPORTANT PART OF CHARLOTTESVILLE. ONCE A PLUSH, REGAL THEATER, ITS FUTURE IS UNKNOWN TODAY. WHILE THE THEATER MAY NOT ENDURE MANY MORE GENERATIONS, TODAY IT STANDS PROUD BASKING IN ITS RICH HISTORY. *PHOTOS BY PHILIP BEAURLINE*

Money Magazine calls one of the international top-20 warm weather summer opera companies. During its nine-week summer run, the Ash Lawn-Highland Summer Festival produces full-length operas and musical theater productions, lectures, Music at Twilight (classical, folk and contemporary music), and Summer Saturdays (family entertainment). For many music lovers, the Summer Festival is a time to pack a gourmet meal, spread a blanket, and enjoy heavenly music amid the soothing surroundings of Monroe's country estate. Over the last few years, the Summer Festival Repertoire has included memorable performances of *Don Giovanni*, *Oklahoma*, *The Marriage of Figaro*, *Camelot*, *Madame Butterfly*, and *The Music Man* to name a few.

For those who enjoy bold, innovative theater there is Live Arts. Located on East Market Street in downtown Charlottesville, Live Arts produces works ranging from new interpretations of classics to avant-garde performance art. Live Arts has been a part of Charlottesville's theater scene since 1990 and runs a full theater season from September to June in its 135-seat Main Space. Live Arts B, which operates out of smaller eighty-seat space, features house workshop productions and individual artists and performers year-round. Live Arts also runs a Summer Theater Festival during the month of July.

The McGuffey Art Center, a co-operative, non-profit organization run by the McGuffey Arts Association, serves as the hub of the artistic community. Located within Charlottesville's downtown historic section, the McGuffey galleries offer the largest displaying space in Charlottesville and the gift shop carries a varied selection of all members' work throughout the year. The McGuffey Art Center is one of many galleries that participate in Charlottesville's traditional "First Friday" art openings in which the public has the opportunity to meet area artists and view their work in a festive atmosphere.

"Charlottesville draws writers the way Nashville beckons to musicians." (*Southern Living*, February 1998). Ranked eighth among top U.S. book markets and number one in avid book reading, Charlottesville is very much a writer's town. In an effort to promote literacy and celebrate reading and books, the Virginia Foundation for the Humanities produces The Virginia Festival of the Book each March. Designed for children and adults, the Festival features hundreds of writers and book related professionals who participate in panel discussions, workshops, and traditional author readings and book signings.

Keeping the public informed about the various arts activities in the region through the course of the year is a function of The Piedmont Council of the Arts (PCA).

The designated arts agency for the city of Charlottesville, Albemarle and surrounding counties, PCA serves more than 50,000 people during the course of a year. The Council has formed partnerships with arts and other community and education organizations to provide ways to extend its outreach programs, promote area artists, and help make the arts available to all citizens.

Increasingly, the University of Virginia is serving as a bridge between the arts and the community by welcoming the public to its programs, lectures, exhibits, and concerts. Thousands of art patrons come to the Bayly Art Museum each year. Servicing both the academic community and the general public, the Museum features ancient art, fifteenth through nineteenth century

AS DIVERSE AS THE UNIVERSITY ITSELF, SO IS THE ART COLLECTION AT THE UNIVERSITY OF VIRGINIA ART MUSEUM (FORMERLY KNOWN AS THE BAYLY ART MUSEUM) LOCATED ON THE UVA.CAMPUS. THE MUSEUM FEATURES CONTEMPORARY AND FOLK ART, UNIQUE SCULPTURES, AND PHOTOGRAPHY. IN ADDITION, THERE IS A PERMANENT COLLECTION OF ARTIFACTS REPRESENTING VARIOUS CULTURES THROUGHOUT THE WORLD. *PHOTO BY PHILIP BEAURLINE*

Also operating under the auspices of the University's Drama Department is The Virginia Film Festival. Nationally recognized for its unique mix of entertainment and education, the Film Festival is the single largest arts event in Charlottesville. For four days during the end of October, the festival brings together directors, actors, scholars, and writers who participate in panel discussions, screenings, and special events based on a theme that illuminates the social and artistic impact of movie making.

Musical performances hosted by The McIntire Department of Music have played to appreciative audiences for years. The seventy-member Charlottesville and University Symphony Orchestra, for instance, perform an outstanding concert subscription season each year. Other ensembles include the U.Va. Jazz Ensemble, University Singers, The Wind & Brass Ensembles, African Drumming & Dance Ensemble, and Early Music Ensemble.

As part of its Virginia 2020 initiative, the University has made a commitment to raise more than $200 million for the Fine and Performing Arts to fulfill an ambitious building and expansion program that will truly transform the cultural life at U.Va. and enable the University to achieve national prominence in the arts.

INCREASINGLY, THE UNIVERSITY OF VIRGINIA IS SERVING AS A BRIDGE BETWEEN THE ARTS AND THE COMMUNITY BY WELCOMING THE PUBLIC TO ITS PROGRAMS, LECTURES, EXHIBITS, AND CONCERTS. THOUSANDS OF ART PATRONS COME TO THE UVA ART MUSEUM EACH YEAR. *PHOTO BY PHILIP BEAURLINE*

American and European paintings and sculpture, Asian art, prints and photographs, and selections from its ethnographic holdings of African, Native American, Oceanic, and pre-Columbian objects. The Museum hosts special exhibitions throughout the year that bring the finest works of art to the Charlottesville area from museums and private collections around the world.

Since 1974, the Heritage Repertory has been the professional repertory theater of U.Va. and the University's Department of Drama. Leading directors, designers, technicians, and actors from across the country join the company each year to produce a season of variety and excellence in repertory theater. In its short seven-week summer season, the Heritage plays to nearly 20,000 people. In addition to the Heritage, the Department of Drama presents 10-12 productions during the September-May academic year.

Included in those plans is the construction of a new Art Museum; a Studio Art Building; a renovated History of Art building; a new music building; expansion of the Drama and the Architecture buildings; a new Fine Arts Library; a new parking garage; and a new 1,500 seat Performing Arts Center for concerts, theater, and dance.

Renovations are happening elsewhere as well. The Paramount Theater, one of the last grand movie palaces, is being painstakingly restored to its original 1931 splendor. Due to open in 2002, the Theater will feature an expanded orchestra pit to accommodate road shows, musicals, dance productions, and other venues in the Performing Arts. With a seating capacity of 1,200 and excellent acoustics, it will be a jewel in Charlottesville's theatrical crown.

Professionals and amateurs alike agree there has never been a better time to be an artist or a patron of the arts than now. Not only has the Charlottesville region become home to the world's most gifted artists, but it also has a growing population of patrons who have the means to support their endeavors. The arts are indeed flourishing in Charlottesville with a future that is as bright as some of the area's rising stars. ■

MUSIC IS AN IMPORTANT AND INSPIRING PART OF THE LIVES OF VIRGINIANS. OAKRIDGE (ABOVE AND RIGHT) SERVES AS A GATHERING PLACE FOR LOCAL MUSICIANS EACH YEAR, AND FOR NEARLY 54 YEARS THE UNIVERSITY OF VIRGINIA HAS INCORPORATED BEAUTIFUL MUSIC INTO EVERYDAY LIVES. THROUGH ITS TUESDAY EVENING MUSIC SERIES, A REGULAR TUESDAY EVENING BECOMES MAGICAL WITH EXTRAORDINARY CONCERTS FEATURING WORLD-RENOWNED CHAMBER MUSICIANS. LOCAL MUSICIANS ALSO GET A CHANCE TO SHOW OFF THEIR RHYTHM AT THE ANNUAL FRIDAYS AFTER 5. HELD EVERY FRIDAY AFTERNOON DURING THE MONTHS OF APRIL THROUGH OCTOBER, THIS EXCITING CONCERT SERIES IS FAVORITE AMONG THE LOCALS. HUNDREDS OF PEOPLE FLOCK TO THE DOWNTOWN MALL TO KICK OFF THEIR WEEKEND AND TAKE IN THE SIGHTS AND SOUNDS OF THE VARIOUS PERFORMERS. *PHOTOS BY PHILIP BEAURLINE*

WITH THE CITY'S MANY MUSIC FESTIVALS, CHORAL GROUPS, AND UNIQUE ENSEMBLES, MUSIC PLAYS AN IMPORTANT ROLE IN THE CULTURE OF CHARLOTTESVILLE. HERE, THE PHOTOGRAPHER'S LONG EXPOSURE OF A LOCAL CHOIR CALLED "BLACK VOICES" CAPTURES THE MOTION OF THE SINGERS AS THEY SWAY BACK AND FORTH SINGING SONGS OF PRAISE. *PHOTO BY PHILIP BEAURLINE*

EDUCATION:
A VISION FOR
LEADERSHIP

■ ■ ■ ■ ■

*"No other sure foundation can be devised for the
preservation of freedom and happiness."*

*—Thomas Jefferson
Letter to George Wythe, 1786*

CONSISTENTLY RANKED AS ONE OF AMERICA'S
TOP UNIVERSITIES, THE UNIVERSITY OF VIRGINIA
IN MANY WAYS EXEMPLIFIES THE STANDARDS
OF EXCELLENCE OF THE ENTIRE LOCAL
EDUCATIONAL SYSTEM. *PHOTO BY
PHILIP BEAURLINE*

Thomas Jefferson passionately believed in the value of public education, so it is not surprising that throughout the region he once called home, there is a high expectation for quality school systems. As a result, people living in the Charlottesville area have a significant number of choices when it comes to educational opportunities. In addition to an acclaimed public school system, the Charlottesville region boasts a number of excellent private schools, ranging from 100-plus year-old institutions to innovative "alternative" schools founded in the last decade. From coeducational boarding and day schools to Catholic and non-denominational Christian schools to a military institute, the Charlottesville region has a generous number of private schools from which to choose.

Having Mr. Jefferson's University in your backyard could be overwhelming to a smaller educational institution, but schools throughout the Charlottesville region look to their neighbor as a resource and benchmark in providing quality educational opportunities for their

CHARLOTTESVILLE BOASTS ONE OF THE MOST WELL-RESPECTED SCHOOL SYSTEMS IN THE NATION. *PHOTO © NOVASTOCK*

students. At U.Va. and other schools, academic tradition is very important. The populace is supportive of all aspects of education, and the strength of local scholastic programs is a testament to the spirit of commitment, dedication, and volunteerism among parents, teachers, and students alike.

The presence of the University of Virginia provides local schools with a pool of highly qualified teachers and enthusiastic volunteers from among its students, graduates, employees, and their spouses. Drawing from their extensive life experiences on both a national and international level, these talented men and women provide area students a global learning perspective. Partnerships between U.Va. and local schools are expanding the use of technology in the classroom, enriching science education, and helping teachers stay up-to-date in a wide range of curricular areas.

Albemarle County Public Schools

Each year, more than one million visitors connect to the Albemarle County Public School System's Web page seeking on-line information about county schools. They are more than pleased in what they discover. A vibrant and diverse school system, Albemarle County public schools provide educational services to more than 12,000 students in 15 elementary schools, five middle schools, and four high schools. In April 2001, *Expansion Magazine* published its tenth annual Educational Quotient national ranking of school districts across the United States. Albemarle County Public Schools received a citation of excellence and a Gold Medal rating, placing the division in the top 17 percent of school divisions in the nation.

"We Expect Success" is the theme of the school system and judging by student performance that goal has been achieved at every level. Students score significantly above national and state averages on national tests when compared to other districts, and more than 80 percent of Albemarle County high school students go on to college. Advancing the academic process of high achieving students is a School Board priority for all county schools. The division is especially proud that 71.5 percent of high school students took the Scholastic Aptitude Test in 1999-2000. The average SAT score in 1999-2000 was 1082, a score that exceeds the state and national average. Of the students who took the SAT, 34 percent scored above 600 on the verbal test and 31 percent scored above 600 on the math test. The number of students participating in Advanced Placement course work has steadily increased in the last decade. In 1999-2000, 788 students were enrolled in one or more of 14 different Advanced Placement courses offered in the county schools. Fifty-nine percent of the high school students graduated with Advanced Studies diplomas, exceeding the state average.

The faculty is exceptionally strong, with a higher percentage of teachers with master's degrees or above than most other school systems. More than 50 percent of the student body participates in some form of athletics, and the arts program nurtures the creativity of students who go on to the Governor's School, as well as into Gifted and AP Programs. Academic programs are supported through low pupil teacher ratios at all levels, a computer density of 1:5, and well-trained teaching assistant staff members. Albemarle County students bring recognition to their schools at the local, state, and national levels. This year, county students have taken top honors in competitions including MathCounts, Math 24, National History Day, Bayly Museum Writer's Eye, and Destination Imagination. The high school band and choral programs have been awarded high competition ratings as exemplified by the Tri-State Best in Class Trophy received by the Western Albemarle Warrior Jazz Band.

Albemarle County schools rate high among parents. Each year the school system conducts a Gallup-type poll designed to measure parent satisfaction. While the national average is 70 percent, county schools receive an 80 percent satisfaction rating from parents, with more than 90 percent indicating their approval of the safety of the schools and the upkeep of the buildings and grounds. Parents and community volunteers are encouraged to become engaged in school activities. In 1999-2000, more than 40,000 hours of volunteer service were recorded across the division. Overall, Albemarle County schools perform in the top 20 percent in the state. This is a reflection of the high standards and overall commitment of the school board, parents, teachers, and students in maintaining a quality school system for all.

While academic achievement is a major goal, Albemarle County schools also are concerned about student character. As an extension of the curriculum, the schools foster an awareness among students toward certain standards and core values. The school system seeks to be all-inclusive and takes a proactive stance when it comes to diversity training among staff, and the promotion of instant reporting when students become victims. The schools operate with an open door policy, encouraging parents and the community at large to participate in programs designed to empower students to rise to their potential.

Charlottesville City Schools

With an average student/classroom teacher ratio of 19:1 for grades K-4, 21:1 for grades 5-6; 18:1 for grades 7-8, and 16.5:1 for grades 9-12, Charlottesville City Schools has one of the best pupil-teacher ratios in the state. City schools have more than 4,000 students who attend six elementary schools (K-4), one upper elementary school (5-6), one middle school (7-8), and one high school (9-12).

In addition to an outstanding academic curriculum, Charlottesville City Schools is dedicated to providing a multitude of support programs and extra-curricular activities to ensure that students have a quality educational experience. The school system is one of the top in the state of Virginia in terms of per-pupil expenditures. This level of financial support enables the schools to offer extensive programs and services to its student body. As a result, excellence can be found in virtually every department.

STUDENTS IN THE CHARLOTTESVILLE REGION SCHOOL SYSTEMS CONSISTENTLY SCORE ABOVE THE NATIONAL AND STATE AVERAGES ON NATIONAL TESTS, AND MAJORITIES GO ON TO ATTEND COLLEGE. STUDENTS ROUTINELY ACHIEVE HONORS IN COMPETITIONS INCLUDING MATHCOUNTS, MATH 24, NATIONAL HISTORY DAY, BAYLY MUSEUM WRITER'S EYE, AND DESTINATION IMAGINATION. *ABOVE PHOTO © WALLY EMERSON. PHOTO BELOW © BILL BACHMANN*

The school system's mission statement places an expectation on students to master a challenging set of academic standards; to find and use information, speak and write effectively, make responsible decisions, and work to achieve personal goals; to appreciate history, diversity, and the achievements of humankind; and to learn to make contributions to the well-being of the community.

To enable them to achieve these goals, the faculty has been chosen carefully to create a healthy balance of new and experienced teachers, with more than 57 percent having advanced degrees. Working together, teachers form a sensitive, responsible relationship with the student body in order to provide everyone with an orderly, focused environment in which to learn.

Charlottesville City Schools are admired for many reasons, but perhaps are best known for their out-standing arts program. Without a doubt, the high school's musical performing groups are the pride of the community, consistently earning top honors in state, national, and even international festivals. The school division has received several prestigious accolades including recognition from The President's Committee on the Arts and the Humanities. In a recent national survey, Charlottesville was ranked #1 in Virginia and thirty-first in the nation as one of the "Best 100 Communities for Music Education in America."

WITH 22 PRIVATE SCHOOLS, CHARLOTTESVILLE PROVIDES STUDENTS WITH MANY EXCEPTIONAL EDUCATIONAL OPPORTUNITIES. PRIVATE SCHOOLS IN THE AREA ARE DENOMINATIONAL AND NON-DENOMINATIONAL AND INCLUDE "ALTERNATIVE" SCHOOLS. BY CATERING TO THE UNIQUE NEEDS OF STUDENTS, PRIVATE SCHOOLS PROVIDE EXCELLENT CURRICULUMS AND EXCITING LEARNING ENVIRONMENTS. *PHOTO © BILL BACHMANN*

WITH A STRONG COMMITMENT FROM STUDENTS, FACULTY, PARENTS, AND VOLUNTEERS, THE CHARLOTTESVILLE SCHOOL SYSTEM PROVIDES STUDENTS WITH THE HIGHEST QUALITY EDUCATION. *PHOTO BY PHILIP BEAURLINE*

Also, Charlottesville has one of the only programs in the state specifically geared to students gifted in the visual arts. Always looking for ways to improve and serve more students, a dance program was recently added to the high school and a string program was initiated in two of the elementary schools.

Teachers hold students to the highest standards of excellence-and it shows! Student concerts, plays, and art exhibits consistently draw large, enthusiastic audiences. The strong emphasis on the arts stems from a division-wide belief that the arts are an intellectual and aesthetic discipline essential for the complete education of every child.

But it's in the academics that the Charlottesville City Schools truly shine. Seventy-five percent of high school students go on to college, with many seniors going to the best universities in the country. SAT Achievement scores in 2000 averaged 1037, higher than both the state and national mean scores. A total of 113 students took 233 different AP tests in May of 2000. Ninety-one percent of these students scored a three or better, and 35 percent of the exams were perfect scores of five. In the spring of 2000, Charlottesville High School had 36 Advanced Placement Scholars. By the spring of 2001, the high school had 14 National Merit Commended Scholars.

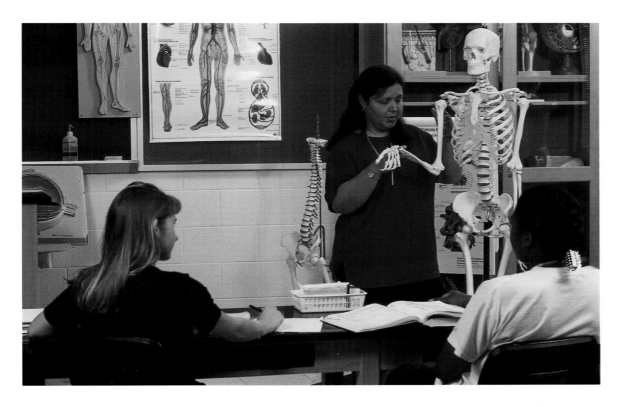

EACH YEAR, THE ALBEMARLE COUNTY SCHOOL SYSTEM CONDUCTS A GALLUP-TYPE POLL DESIGNED TO MEASURE PARENT SATISFACTION. WHILE THE NATIONAL AVERAGE IS 70 PERCENT, COUNTY SCHOOLS RECEIVE AN 80-PERCENT SATISFACTION RATING FROM PARENTS, WITH MORE THAN 90 PERCENT INDICATING THEIR APPROVAL OF THE SAFETY OF THE SCHOOLS AND THE UPKEEP OF THE BUILDINGS AND GROUNDS. *PHOTO © BILL BACHMANN*

Charlottesville Albemarle Technical Education Center

The Charlottesville Albemarle Technical Education Center (CATEC) is a secondary and post-secondary career and technical training center co-owned by Charlottesville and Albemarle school divisions. CATEC offers academic, career, and technical education programs for high school students in Charlottesville, Albemarle, and Fluvanna Counties. CATEC offers courses in Information Technology (Computer Networking, Repair & Maintenance, Multi-Media, TV & Video Production); Health & Medical Services (Health Careers, Laboratory Animal Technician, Certified Nursing Assistant); Construction Technology (Carpentry, Electrical, Masonry); Automotive Technology (Auto Collision Repair, Auto Body Prep and Service Technology); Human and Public Services (Cosmetology, Culinary Arts, and Early Childhood Education); and Integrated Academics (English, Math, U.S. Government, GED Program).

CATEC was established in 1973, a time when the federal government realized that schools were not providing the trained workforce needed to meet the changing needs of employers nationwide. As a result, the government established the Carl Perkins Fund for high school vocational training programs. In Virginia, several localities, such as the Charlottesville/Albemarle area, combined resources to create a regional center thereby allowing students from multiple high schools to come to one training site. Today there are 10 regional centers in Virginia, including the 57,000 square-foot facility on East Rio Road in Charlottesville.

As the face of regional employment is changing from manufacturing to technology, so is the face of CATEC. Classes dealing with electronics, welding, machine tool and die were replaced by information technology, video and multi-media production. Today CATEC is the regional administration site and provider of apprenticeship training for regional businesses. CATEC also serves as the administrative agent for the Charlottesville Public Schools Adult Education Program.

Typically, CATEC students spend a half-day at their high school and a half-day receiving technical training at CATEC. The majority of CATEC's vocational teachers come from the business community to teach students the skills and trades they need to enter the workplace. In the end, CATEC's goal is to provide people with the skills they need to positively impact their lives, obtain employment, and develop rewarding, professional careers.

THE SCHOOL SYSTEM'S MISSION STATEMENT PLACES AN
EXPECTATION ON STUDENTS TO MASTER A CHALLENGING SET OF
ACADEMIC STANDARDS; TO FIND AND USE INFORMATION, SPEAK
AND WRITE EFFECTIVELY, MAKE RESPONSIBLE DECISIONS, AND
WORK TO ACHIEVE PERSONAL GOALS; TO APPRECIATE HISTORY,
DIVERSITY, AND THE ACHIEVEMENTS OF HUMANKIND; AND TO
LEARN TO MAKE CONTRIBUTIONS TO THE WELL-BEING OF THE
COMMUNITY. *PHOTO BY PHILIP BEAURLINE*

Piedmont Virginia Community College

Piedmont Virginia Community College (PVCC) is a
two-year state-supported commuter college that is one
of 23 in the Virginia Community College System. PVCC
is well respected, both within the Charlottesville region
and beyond, for its track record in college transfer and
workforce preparation. The college enrolls more than
4,000 students each semester, representing nearly 50
percent of all residents in the region who are attending
college in Virginia.

Many students come to PVCC for the first two
years of baccalaureate study. They benefit because the
college is close to home, is affordable, and allows for
part-time study so they can work while attending college. Additionally, the excellent instruction provided by
a knowledgeable and dedicated faculty prepares students
well for transfer to a four-year college or university.

PVCC is particularly proud of its relationship with the
University of Virginia. Since the college opened in 1972,
more than 1,500 students have transferred to U.Va.,
earning grade point averages and graduation rates
equal to those of students who enroll in the university
as first-year students.

The Charlottesville region has come to rely on
PVCC for workforce programs. The college works with
employers to ensure that students who enroll in workforce programs learn the skills they need to advance
on the job. In many cases, the college partners with
area employers to develop specific programs to address
particular workforce needs. Programs in financial
accounting, surgical technology, biotechnology,
insurance and web design are examples of these
employer-sponsored ventures. PVCC is a partner in
Charlottesville's Connected Community Technology
Center, providing college opportunities in the downtown area and helping the community address the
issue of the digital divide.

As the college looks to the future, it will continue
to link with employers to provide workforce programs
that support a 21st Century economy. It will develop
expanded community programming in the visual and
performing arts in its new V. Earl Dickinson Building.
And it will look for ways to harness the power of the
world wide Web and other technologies to bring
courses to students at the time and place of their
choosing, thus making quality higher education
accessible to all.

Charlottesville Area School Business Alliance

Founded in 1996, local businesses teamed up with
the Albemarle, Charlottesville, and Fluvanna County
Public Schools and the Charlottesville Regional
Chamber of Commerce to form The Charlottesville
Area School Alliance (CASBA) to explore new ways to
ensure that youth leave high school prepared to be
successful in post-secondary education and/or the
workforce. Among CASBA programs are Career Fairs
for seventh and tenth graders where students gather
information about specific careers and the workplace
in general; Project RE-SEED, which prepares retired
engineers and scientists to assist middle school teachers
with science experiments and demonstrations; the
annual Regional Job Fair, which brings together
employers, job seekers, and their parents to explore
summer, part-time, or permanent employment; the
Business Educator Exchange Program, a five-day
observation and research experience at the business site
to enable educators to increase their understanding of
the skills, knowledge, and attitudes needed by students
for successful employment; and the Summer Internship
Program, which partners students with local businesses
where they work for the summer as a paid intern.

YEAR AFTER YEAR, THE UNIVERSITY OF VIRGINIA HAS BEEN CHOSEN BY A NUMBER OF MAGAZINES AND ORGANIZATIONS AS ONE OF THE TOP UNIVERSITIES IN THE COUNTRY. MOST RECENTLY, UVA AND THE UNIVERSITY OF CALIFORNIA-BERKELEY TIED AS THE NATION'S #1 PUBLIC UNIVERSITY IN THE FOURTEENTH ANNUAL "AMERICA'S BEST COLLEGES" ISSUE OF *U.S. NEWS & WORLD REPORT* (SEPTEMBER 2000). *PHOTO BY PHILIP BEAURLINE*

University of Virginia

When Thomas Jefferson founded his "academical village" in 1819, he envisioned it as an institution "based on the illimitable freedom of the human mind, to explore and to expose every subject susceptible of its contemplation." (letter to Destutt de Tracy, December 26, 1820). The school has more than lived up to Mr. Jefferson's ideals.

The University opened its doors to 68 students in 1825; Thomas Jefferson was its first Rector. By 2001, student enrollment was 18,550, representing all 50 states and 75 foreign countries. Of the 12,489 undergraduate students, two-thirds are Virginia residents. Admission is highly competitive. U.Va. students exemplify Jefferson's vision for well-prepared leaders who will go on to help shape the future of the nation. They possess intellectual ability and academic achievement as well as evidence of good character, imagination, leadership, facility in self-expression, commitment to service, and other qualities that contribute to the University and local community.

Students need only look to U.Va.'s esteemed list of alumni for role models. Past and present political leaders include President Woodrow Wilson; Senators Robert and Edward Kennedy; John Warner, Charles Robb, and Christopher "Kit" Bond; Congressman L.F. Payne; and Governors James Gilmore, George Allen, Gerald Baliles, B. Evan Bayh III, Angus King, and Lowell Weicker. In the arts, famous University graduates include Louis Auchincloss, Lewis Allen (the Broadway producer of *Annie*), Mark Johnson (the movie producer of *Rain Man* and *Good Morning, Vietnam*), Henry Taylor (the 1986 Pulitzer Price winner for poetry), and Edgar Allan Poe. Other notable alumni include astronauts Kathryn Thornton and Karl Heinze, State Supreme Court Justices Leroy B. Hassell and John Charles Thomas, medical pioneer Walter Reed, Palestinian spokeswoman Hanan Ashrawi, and broadcast journalist Katherine Couric.

Over the years, the University of Virginia has been chosen by a number of prestigious magazines and organizations as one of the top schools in the country. In its 14th annual "America's Best Colleges" issue (September 2000), *U.S. News & World Report* ranked U.Va. the nation's #1 public university in a tie with the University of California-Berkeley. In addition, some of the University's undergraduate schools, graduate schools and programs, and hospital specialties were chosen as among the nation's best. In 1995, the renowned National Research Council, which evaluates 275 institutions once every 10 years, placed U.Va.'s graduate programs high on the list. In September 2000, *Kiplinger's Magazine* ranked the University of Virginia as the #2 Best Quality Public College/University based on a combination of quality, cost, and financial aid measures. And Solucient named the University's Medical Center as one of the nation's Top 100 Hospitals for the third year in a row.

Jefferson personally selected the original faculty of eight professors, including noted young scholars from European universities. Today, the University of Virginia's distinguished faculty consists of more than 1,900 full-time scholars, including the former Poet Laureate of the United States, several Pulitzer Prize winners, and 23 Guggenheim fellows to name a few. Their ground-breaking work attracts millions of dollars each year in research funding. External funding for fiscal year 2000 surpassed $209 million in support from federal and state agencies and private foundations. Research in the humanities and programs in the biomedical, physical, and engineering sciences are among the areas of strength at the University of Virginia. New research instrumentation exceeds $10 million each year. With estimated total revenues for 2000-01 at $1.3 billion, The University of Virginia is one of only three public universities awarded a bond rating of "AA+" by Standard and Poor's, Aaa by Moody's Investors Service, and AAA by Fitch.

The University of Virginia has 10 schools; five of the 10-Architecture, Arts and Sciences, the McIntire School of Commerce, Engineering and Applied Sciences, and Nursing-offer both undergraduate and graduate studies. The Darden Graduate School of Business

Administration, the School of Law, and the School of Medicine offer graduate studies. The Curry School of Education offers graduate degrees and a five-year dual degree program with the College of Arts and Sciences through which students receive both an undergraduate degree and a master's in teaching. The School of Continuing and Professional Studies offers a part-time undergraduate degree and many other programs and graduate study. These schools are supported by a vast library system that holds four million volumes, as well as one of the world's largest electronic text libraries, and a valuable collection of rare books and manuscripts.

A member of the highly competitive Atlantic Coast Conference, the University of Virginia fields 12 inter-collegiate sports for men and 12 for women. U.Va. ranked 13th in the nation in the final 1999-2000 Sears Directors' Cup standings, which rank the overall success of Division I athletic programs in up to 20 sports.

Jefferson waged a tireless "campaign against igno-rance," believing that "knowledge is power, knowledge is safety, and knowledge is happiness." True to Jefferson's vision, the University of Virginia serves as the democratic proving ground for leadership. That vision has become a driving force in both public and private schools throughout the Charlottesville region. Today, more than 180 years after its founding, the University of Virginia remains the crown jewel in Charlottesville's educational, social, political, and economic life. ∎

"**P**eople can count on the University's presence. It has been here since 1819 and, as a major residential research university, with a teaching hospital, will continue to be the region's largest employer. There may be bumps in the road with state funding and other kinds of things, but our research enterprise is growing. The rule of thumb is that for every million dollars in new research money, 35 jobs are created, either directly as a part of that research project, or indirectly, in support of the project. This is one important way we contribute to our local economy here and to job opportunities for Virginians."

Louise M. Dudley
Assistant Vice President for University Relations
University of Virginia

TODAY, MORE THAN 180 YEARS AFTER IT'S FOUNDING, THE UNIVERSITY OF VIRGINIA REMAINS THE CROWN JEWEL IN CHARLOTTESVILLE'S EDUCATIONAL, SOCIAL, POLITICAL, AND ECONOMIC LIFE. *PHOTOS BY PHILIP BEAURLINE*

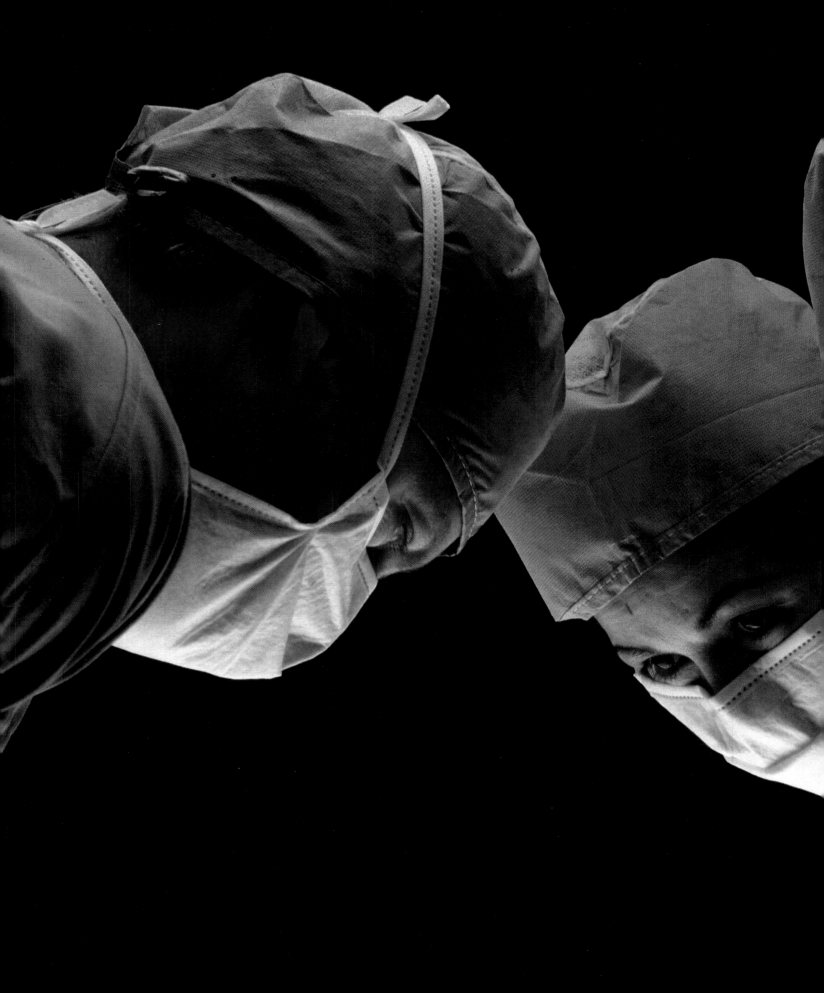

7 | CHAPTER SEVEN

HEALTH CARE—
SIMPLY THE BEST

· · · · · ·

"Without health there is no happiness.
An attention to health, then, should take place
of every other object."

—Thomas Jefferson
Letter to T.M. Randolph, Jr., 1787

RATED AMONG THE BEST IN THE NATION, THE
HEALTH CARE SYSTEMS IN CHARLOTTESVILLE ARE
TRULY EXCEPTIONAL. MARTHA JEFFERSON
HOSPITAL AND THE UNIVERSITY OF VIRGINIA
HEALTH SYSTEM HAVE BOTH BEEN NAMED TO
THE LIST OF TOP 100 HOSPITALS IN THE COUNTRY.
THE HIGH ACCESSIBILITY TO TOP-NOTCH HEALTH
CARE REMAINS A DECIDING FACTOR FOR PEOPLE
CONSIDERING MOVING TO CHARLOTTESVILLE.
WITH SKILLED PHYSICIANS AND NURSES AND
STATE-OF-THE-ART RESEARCH AND TECHNOLOGY,
THE HOSPITALS PROVIDE THE FINEST HEALTH CARE
TREATMENT IN VIRGINIA. *PHOTO © DON WOLF.*

For a community of its size, the Charlottesville region enjoys the rare distinction of having two excellent choices for health care: the University of Virginia Health System, one of the most revered academic medical centers in the country; and Martha Jefferson Hospital, providing comprehensive community care. Even more rare is the fact that both have been named among the Top 100 Hospitals in the country. Coupled with numerous outpatient locations for patient convenience provided by both hospitals, Charlottesville area residents can get treatment for virtually any disorder without having to travel long distances. With world-class physicians, extensive research programs, and comprehensive services, it is no wonder that accessibility to health care in the Charlottesville region is a major draw for people deciding to move into the area.

The University of Virginia Health System

Although Thomas Jefferson recruited Dr.Robley Dunglison, a world-renowned physician from England, to begin the University of Virginia's medical school and patient care program in 1825, it wasn't until the spring of 1901 that the University actually dedicated its first hospital: a 25-bed building with three operating rooms. Built for $50,000 in a vacant field just east of the academic area, the hospital was ideally located less than a mile from the busy C&O Railway Station on Main Street where patients and their families arrived daily on one of 30 trains that stopped at the station.

Today people travel from around the world to avail themselves of the highly sophisticated primary care and specialty services delivered at this nationally acclaimed academic medical center. The Health System includes a 591-bed hospital, numerous clinics on the U.Va. campus and at more than 40 locations throughout Charlottesville and neighboring counties, a network of almost 600 physicians who provide every level of medical care, an extensive library, and outstanding Medical and Nursing schools.

The University of Virginia Health System is known for its specialized care and world-class physicians who offer coordinated treatment through centers focused in specific areas. The Cancer Center brings together multi-disciplinary specialists who offer some of the most

UVA MEDICAL CENTER (HEALTH SYSTEM)- THE UNIVERSITY OF VIRGINIA HEALTH SYSTEM PROVIDES SPECIALIZED TREATMENT FOR A NUMBER OF ILLNESSES. FROM THE CHILDREN'S MEDICAL CENTER TO THE CENTER FOR ADULT REHABILITATION, THE HEALTH SYSTEM OFFERS CUTTING-EDGE FACILITIES THAT SPECIALIZE IN HEART, CANCER, DIGESTIVE, NEUROSCIENCE, AND WOMEN'S HEALTH CARE. IN ADDITION, IT COMBINES AN EXCELLENT STAFF OF DOCTORS, NURSES, AND SUPPORT STAFF TO CAREFULLY ATTEND TO THE DELICATE NEEDS OF ITS PATIENTS. *PHOTO BY PHILIP BEAURLINE*

advanced treatments available for all types of cancer. Renowned cardiologists, surgeons, cardiac nurses, physical therapists, and other health professionals work together at The Heart Center to offer a continuum of care, from prevention, diagnosis, and drug therapies to surgery, transplant, and rehabilitation. The Digestive Health Center features experts in gastroenterology, surgery, radiology, psychiatry, and other areas, while The Neurosciences Service Center provides coordinated care for patients with neurological diseases and injury, including stroke, epilepsy, degenerative diseases, brain tumors, neonatal and developmental disorders, and other neurological problems. The Women's Place combines a wide range of programs to address the health concerns affecting a woman at every stage of her life, and The Children's Medical Center provides a comprehensive network of health care services dedicated to the care of children from birth through adolescence. And for seniors, there is The Center for Adult Rehabilitation and Elder Care (CARE), featuring university physicians and nurses who are specially trained in geriatric health.

Now entering its second century of care, the Health System remains one of the most innovative and cutting-edge health care facilities in the country. Considered a Level 1 Trauma Center, the Emergency Department provides treatment for all types of medical emergencies and features air ambulance service and a chest pain center for the rapid diagnosis of heart problems. The hospital's extensive research program enables patients and the public to participate in clinical trials and have access to medical technology in its development stage, a capability that has been proven to save lives. And the Health Sciences Library provides up-to-date information and research findings to hospitals, doctors, nurses, and pharmacists throughout the area. Remaining on top of the information highway has enabled the hospital to be the first in the state to offer new medical procedures, products, or services to the community when they become available and then share this knowledge with the public through regularly scheduled free health care classes.

Each year, the nation's brightest medical students enroll in The University of Virginia School of Medicine, attracted in part by the fact that the school has one of the most distinguished faculty in the country. An impressive endowment of more than $120 million in annual grants has supported the faculty in its quest for new and better therapies for patients, especially in the areas of cardiovascular disease, neurodegenerative and endocrine diseases, and vaccine development. Like the School of Medicine, the University of Virginia School of Nursing enjoys a national reputation for excellence in education, research, and practice and is ranked among the top 25 public nursing schools in the country.

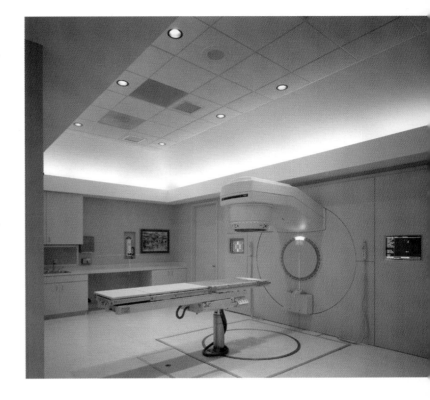

WHEN IT COMES TO QUALITY HEALTH CARE, CHARLOTTESVILLE RESIDENTS DON'T HAVE TO LOOK FAR. WITH TWO MAJOR HOSPITALS AND A NUMBER OF OUTPATIENT AND PHYSICIAN SERVICES IN THE AREA, WORLD-CLASS TREATMENT IS RIGHT IN THEIR BACK YARD. AND FOR THOSE NOT LIVING IN CHARLOTTESVILLE, THE HEALTH CARE SYSTEM PROVIDES CLINICS IN NEIGHBORING COUNTIES. BY COVERING HEALTH CARE IN CHARLOTTESVILLE AND BEYOND, THE HEALTH CARE SYSTEM IS AS ACCESSIBLE AS IT IS SUCCESSFUL. *PHOTO BY PHILIP BEAURLINE*

The Health System has more than 4,400 full-time employees with 1,100 volunteers putting in close to 71,000 volunteer hours. The staff is known for its genuine caring, warmth, and compassion, concerned with both the patient's physical and emotional well being. In that regard, the Health System provides an impressive network of support services, including chaplains and social workers, which provide a depth of backup that is not available at smaller institutions. A strong collaboration exists between the medical and surgical specialties, radiology, and pathology. Patients entering the Health System with a specific problem are attended to by a team of doctors, nurses, social workers, and other health care professionals who explore all avenues of care for that patient.

The University of Virginia Health System was named among the 100 Top Hospitals in the country for three years in a row by Solucient and since 1989 has been named by U.S. News & World Report as one of America's Best Hospitals.

WITH ITS 180 LICENSED BEDS, MARTHA JEFFERSON HOSPITAL MAY NOT BE BIG IN SIZE, BUT YOU WOULDN'T KNOW THAT JUDGING BY HOW THE HOSPITAL IMPACTS THE HEALTH OF THOSE LIVING IN THE CHARLOTTESVILLE REGION. THE HOSPITAL AND ITS PHYSICIANS SET THE STANDARD FOR QUALITY, COST-EFFECTIVE COMMUNITY HEALTHCARE. *PHOTO BY PHILIP BEAURLINE*

Martha Jefferson Hospital

Shortly after the University of Virginia opened its ward-style hospital, a group of physicians saw the need to form a different type of hospital, one that would serve people of moderate means who preferred to be treated as private patients. Among the founders was Dr. William M. Randolph, a descendant of Jefferson's daughter Martha, who named the hospital after his famous ancestor.

Originally called "The Martha Jefferson Sanatorium Association, Inc." the name was changed in November 1917 to "Martha Jefferson Hospital, Inc." When the hospital opened in July 1904, it was estimated an average of eight patients a day would pay expenses. The charge for a semi-private bed was $14 a week and private rooms were $15-20 per week. Dr. Browning, one of the founders, performed the first operation, "an emergency appendectomy." Since then, the hospital has grown from a small sanitorium to a facility that sits on nine acres of land in downtown Charlottesville. In the spring of 2001, Martha Jefferson Hospital acquired 84 acres of land at I-64 and Route 250, east of Charlottesville, and announced plans for expansion of its facilities and services for its second hundred years.

From the beginning, the desire to provide personal care has been a part of the Martha Jefferson tradition. The hospital is very progressive in keeping up with changes in health care delivery, emphasizing not only patient quality of care, but easy access and convenience. Patients receive the latest in cancer therapies at the Cancer Care Center, including medical, surgical, and radiation oncology. Emphasizing the whole person, the Martha Jefferson cancer treatment program also provides complementary therapies and educational resources. With comprehensive diagnostic procedures to a full range of rehabilitation and health education programs, the doctors, nurses, pharmacists, and technologists of the Cardiology Care Center work together as a team to build a customized care plan for each individual. Vascular Interventional Radiology at Martha Jefferson Hospital uses the latest medical imaging technology and the skill of specially trained radiologists to detect and treat vascular disorders, without surgery in many cases. Martha Jefferson's Women's Health Center provides family-centered maternity care, including the Prenatal Diagnosis Center that offers the earliest screenings possible for abnormalities in unborn babies. A wide choice of physicians and a comprehensive range of pre- and post-natal education and support programs make Martha Jefferson a popular choice for new families. Programs for midlife women include hormone replacement therapy, migraines, osteoporosis,

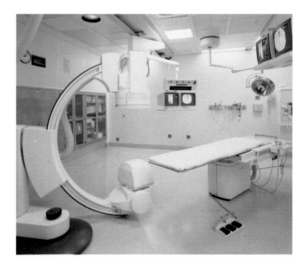

BY COMBINING THE NEWEST MEDICAL TECHNOLOGY WITH A CARING STAFF, HEALTH CARE SYSTEMS IN CHARLOTTESVILLE ARE AMONG THE BEST. THE TECHNOLOGY USED TO DIAGNOSE AND TREAT ILLNESSES IS THE LATEST AND MOST INNOVATIVE. IN ORDER TO KEEP UP WITH THE IMPROVEMENTS MADE BY SCIENCE, THE TECHNOLOGICAL RESOURCES ARE CONSTANTLY BEING UPDATED. HEALTH CARE SYSTEMS ARE ABLE TO GIVE PATIENTS THE BEST POSSIBLE CARE BY PROVIDING A WEALTH OF SPECIALIZED EQUIPMENT AND PRACTICES. *PHOTO BY PHILIP BEAURLINE*

nutrition, and breast care. The Digestive Care Center relies on several medical disciplines and state-of-the-art capabilities to evaluate and treat gastrointestinal and motility disorders, liver disease, and pancreatic and biliary duct disorders.

Martha Jefferson has 11 outpatient sites throughout the community, 10 of which have a primary care physician practice in addition to diagnostic capabilities. In medical practices where primary care physicians are on staff, the hospital brings mobile mammography to each of those office sites, giving women the opportunity to have a mammogram without having to travel great distances.

Martha Jefferson Hospital employs 1,500 employees and has a very active group of volunteers, including its highly regarded Women's Committee made up of 100 dedicated volunteers. Since its inception in 1994, the Women's Committee's goal has been to provide access to quality breast health care for all women. To date, the Committee has raised more than $650,000 in support of Martha Jefferson Hospital's community breast cancer and breast health outreach programs through its annual award-winning fundraising event, Martha's Market, which has become a Charlottesville tradition.

With its 180 licensed beds, Martha Jefferson Hospital may not be big in size, but you wouldn't know that judging by how the hospital impacts the health of those living in the Charlottesville region. The hospital and its

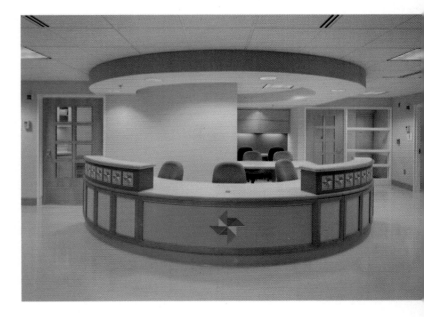

FROM THE EARLIEST STAGES OF LIFE TO THE LATEST, CHARLOTTESVILLE'S MEDICALFACILITIES EFFECTIVELY CONTRIBUTE TO RAISING THE QUALITY OF LIFE FOR ALL RESIDENTS. *PHOTOS BY PHILIP BEAURLINE*

physicians set the standard for quality, cost-effective community healthcare. As they were with the founding of the hospital a century ago, Martha Jefferson Hospital physicians continue to be actively involved with the hospital in continuously improving clinical quality as well as the quality of the patient's experience. Martha Jefferson physicians play an essential role on the hospital board that is comprised of six physicians and six lay people. With this type of representation, physicians have a hands-on part in making all decisions at Martha Jefferson, from constructing a building to buying a new piece of equipment.

A model community healthcare system, Martha Jefferson Hospital's mission is to serve as a community resource in raising the health status of area residents. It does this in several ways, including the Community Health Partnership Program, health information centers such as HealthSource Library, the Cancer Care Resource Center, free community health education programs, and health screenings.

Recognized by Solucient, Martha Jefferson Hospital was named as one of the top 100 hospitals in the nation based upon excellence in quality of care, efficiency of operations, and sustainability of overall performance. Martha Jefferson Hospital has been accredited by the Joint Commission for the Accreditation of Health Care Organizations, and its Cancer Care Center has been designated a Community Hospital Comprehensive Cancer Care Center by the American College of Surgeons Commission on Cancer. ■

CHAPTER EIGHT

THE FUTURE OF THE CHARLOTTESVILLE REGION

. . . . .

"I like the dreams of the future better than the history of the past."

—*Thomas Jefferson*
Letter to John Adams, 1816

Within the hearts and minds of every soul exists a vision of what the coming years will bring. Those fortunate enough to call the Charlottesville region their home view the future as a sacred trust. Cognizant of the cultural and historical richness of the area, blessed by incomparable beauty and limitless opportunities, Charlottesvillians have become stewards of a treasured way of life they know must be preserved for future generations. With this awesome responsibility ever present on the minds of leading businessmen, elected officials, educators, and cultural leaders, their perspective on the future of the Charlottesville region provides a fascinating glimpse of things to come.

Blake Caravati, Mayor of the City of Charlottesville, anticipates Charlottesville will be a "world-class city":

"Charlottesville has the deserved reputation as one of the best places in the country to live, work, play, retire, and

PHOTO BY PHILIP BEAURLINE

raise a family. Our City's efforts and resources have been directed toward building upon this reputation by providing our children with the best progressive education possible, improving our neighborhoods through resourceful planning, and encouraging environmentally friendly high-tech economic development in our business corridors, including the heart of our City, the Downtown Pedestrian Mall.

"Charlottesville is blessed with natural beauty, a rich history, a diversity of people and ideas, and with careful planning we can insure that every citizen has the opportunity to share in our City's bright future. Our government and all of our citizens view our future with great optimism and are working hard to make Charlottesville "A World Class City".

John Casteen, President of the University of Virginia, envisions the University will achieve ambitious goals by the year 2020:

"Our goal is to see to it that the University of Virginia remains the top public institution in the country and that it ranks within the nation's top 10 or 15 overall. The goal is not to say foolishly that we intend to displace Cal Tech or Harvard. It is that we intend to be in the neighborhood, in a competitive position, having cultivated selected areas of unparalleled eminence. We intend to remain relatively small by comparison to other major institutions and residential because we believe that in the life of students on these Grounds lies part of the essential value of education here. And we intend to expand our commitment to public service both locally and throughout the Commonwealth.

"When all is said and done, the University's most important investment for the future is not in its buildings, in its history, or its Grounds. The investment is in students and in faculty and in staff.

"There is a Chinese proverb that speaks to what we do. It goes: "If you are planning for one year, grow rice. If you are planning for twenty years, grow trees. If you are planning for centuries, grow people."

Michael Gaffney, President of Gaffney Homes and 2001 Chair-Elect of the Charlottesville Regional Chamber of Commerce, believes Charlottesville will continue to be one of the top places to live in the country:

"In the year 2021, I believe the Greater Charlottesville area will continue to make everyone's Top 10 List of Best Places To Live, reflecting the natural beauty of the mountains and the countryside, the leisure offerings of golf, hiking, bicycling, and canoeing, and the friendliness of the inhabitants. The University will continue to be the single-most named attraction with the Hospital, the Research Parks and the Retirement Communities always mentioned.

"The growth of business, retail shopping and new residential communities will be interwoven within designated areas of growth that will radiate along the major arteries

and into the surrounding counties which will become an integral part of the community. Commercial and industrial areas, having been built within the master plans, will minimize road congestion and afford people short drives to work of less than 15 minutes.

"In the next 20 years, I believe the Charlottesville region will have achieved its goal of reasonable growth while retaining the beauty and livability of the area for all residents."

For Daniel P. Jordan, President of the Thomas Jefferson Foundation, the realization of Jefferson's vision for education can become the hallmark of the Charlottesville region:

"While no one can predict the future, we all have aspirations for it. Some area residents work for an economic culture that lessens the disparity between the truly prosperous and those who struggle for a livelihood. Others seek to preserve the rural character of the area, including its magnificent open spaces and historic resources. Still others look forward to a constructive public discourse where officials and citizens debate complex and emotional issues in a tone of civility.

"For me, one vision of the future transcends all others. I hope that twenty years from now the Charlottesville-Albemarle region will stand as the national model for public education. As Jefferson repeatedly argued, 'If the condition of man is to be progressively ameliorated...education is to be the chief instrument in effecting it.' Wouldn't it be wonderful if the nation's premier public schools were in this area? If the University of Virginia expanded its outreach programs and commitment to life-long learning to encompass truly the entire community? If public television and local Internet resources worked together on educational initiatives? If teachers were given greater respect, higher compensation, and more authority over their classrooms and time with students?

"Education has an unequaled potential for improving our society and achieving our wish list of dreams. As Jefferson wisely reminded us long ago, "I think by far the most important bill in our whole code is that for the diffusion of knowledge...No other sure foundation can be devised for the preservation of freedom and happiness."

Gary O'Connell, Charlottesville City Manager, foresees the area continuing to thrive in all areas:

"The future success of the Charlottesville region is contingent upon our ability to capitalize on our strong local economy without losing sight of the importance of the many quality of life issues that currently make Charlottesville a wonderful place to live. Our vision of Charlottesville 20 years from now is a City that's thriving with high-tech environmentally sound companies, producing well educated children, and providing culturally enriching experiences while maintaining our aura as a small, friendly

PHOTO BY PHILIP BEAURLINE

urban area. With the right mix of planning and citizen empowerment there is little doubt that we can accomplish our goals."

Robert W. Tucker, Jr., Albemarle County Executive, predicts today's positive trends will continue into the future:

"As I envision our Albemarle County and Charlottesville region in the upcoming years, I see several trends that provide us with numerous opportunities to continue our reputation as a progressive and prosperous community. We will continue to face the challenge of meeting the pressures of growth and development, which stem from our desirability as a residential and business location while we strive to preserve the historic, cultural, and natural resources that define our sense of place. Our designated development areas will take a denser, more urban like form with increased amenities as we work to channel the majority of growth away from our rural areas and into concentrated centers of development.

"New technological advances will provide us with increased avenues for communicating with and interacting with our citizens and will help us develop links that connect us as a community. I envision a more networked region physically as well as electronically as we resolve and move ahead with critical links in our transportation system including the development of alternative forms of transportation that complement our new urban environments. Our region will continue to evolve as a vital, thriving area capable of meeting the demands of a growing and diversifying population."

Cathy Smith Train, President United Way-Thomas Jefferson Area, is confident that people in the Charlottesville area will continue to generously support social programs:

"Charlottesville and the surrounding area offer a rich and rewarding life for many. The United Way-Thomas Jefferson Area's work and hope is that through the philanthropic efforts of local citizens in collaboration with community health and human service agencies and local government,

services are available that support local residents in need as they care for and nurture their children, that enable them to access health care, education, and employment opportunities, and more. With the availability of these services and this support, every individual and family living in our community will experience the quality of life we all hold so dear."

Delegate Mitchell Van Yahres, 57th House District, Virginia House of Delegates expects viable solutions for future transportation issues:

"The future of the Charlottesville/Albemarle region will depend on how we address the increasing problem of population mobility. We will have to utilize land use planning and flexible integrated mass transit systems as a means of reducing dependence on the automobile. I believe that our region will work together to deal with our transportation problems by developing a system that incorporates busses, vanpools, and other innovative options. This transit system will be accessible to low income residents both in terms of physical location and the frequency. By reducing dependency on the automobile we will increase job opportunities and make affordable housing more accessible and realistic."

And Aubrey Watts, Director of Economic Development for City of Charlottesville, is confident the area's economy will continue to grow:

"The region's steady, stable economy will continue to be somewhat of an anomaly in that it will not depend on a traditional large employer base, but rather on an unusually high 88 percent small business sector. The fastest growing segments of business development within the City of Charlottesville will continue to be the high-technology industry. This factor, coupled with the presence of the University and a thriving tourist trade, will continue to make the area less vulnerable to recession and the "boom-to-bust" economic swings that plague other communities. Charlottesville's emphasis on mixed development with residential, business, and retail centers being combined in a coordinated site will transform the downtown area from a 9 to 5 work center into a vibrant 24-hour community. After researching the area, many young-at-heart entrepreneurs who, in the past retired here for the golf and leisure activities, will begin to find the Charlottesville region ideal for starting second careers and will invest their money into developing new businesses that add to the wealth and value of the community at large."

Whatever the future holds for the Charlottesville region, those already living here and those who will soon someday call this area home are entrusted with a sacred responsibility: to treasure and perpetuate a way of life that has nurtured and inspired generations for more than 200 years. ■

PHOTOS BY PHILIP BEAURLINE

PHOTO BY PHILIP BEAURLINE

PHOTO BY PHILIP BEAURLINE

GAFFNEY HOMES

■ ■ ■ ■ ■

When people are asked what is the biggest frustration they face in building a new home, they often say it's finding a team of talented, dedicated people who embrace their dream and help shape it into reality. Gaffney Homes is such a team and Mike Gaffney often tells how it came about:

"In 1974, Lenny Riggio redirected my life from one of large company employee to entrepreneur in a matter of minutes. Lenny started with a basement storefront with his partner supplying funds from his yogurt truck. By the time I met him, he had already created a chain of 20 college book stores built around innovation, risk taking, great vision, and dedicated employees.

"He painted a future that I could envision and adopt as my own. I saw how he attracted energetic and dynamic people that would change the face of his industry. He treated us as partners and friends, and rewarded us based on our value to the company. In turn, we were extremely dedicated and loyal and worked harder for Lenny than anyone could imagine. Those qualities became a part of me, part of the experience of our customers, and the people we managed who joined us in bringing Lenny's vision to life in Barnes & Noble.

WRAP-AROUND PORCH AND FINE ARCHITECTURAL DETAILING ARE FEATURES OF THIS TRADITIONAL VIRGINIA HOME IN THE WALNUT HILL COMMUNITY. GAFFNEY HOMES HAS BUILT IN MANY OF THE CHARLOTTESVILLE AREA'S MOST ELEGANT NEIGHBORHOODS.

"I had many goals at that time, but this experience compelled me to create a company of my own with those same attributes. It would be 10 years before I discovered that homebuilding created the fire in me that I saw in Lenny. Gaffney Homes is a product of that fire."

Mike Gaffney built his first home in 1987 and the evolution began. His business philosophy can best be described as: Building With Integrity. And integrity is something that can be seen in every aspect of Gaffney Homes: from personalized customer service, to unparalleled professionalism in design and construction of each new home. Gaffney Homes is a dedicated group of individuals working as a team to bring the best experience in home building to their customers. "We measure ourselves against the highest values of honesty, fairness, thoroughness, patience, compassion, and commitment to improvement," Gaffney explains. "Our dedication and loyalty to each customer comes through every day in our work. We realize we are creating more than just a home. This is where our clients build a lifetime of family memories."

As an active member of the Charlottesville Regional Chamber of Commerce, Mike Gaffney shares the desire of other local business leaders to improve the living experience of all citizens.

"We are committed to helping create the best place in the world to live. Not only do we build great homes and neighborhoods, we also volunteer and actively participate in local organizations that preserve the beauty and enhance the quality of life in the Charlottesville area."

OWNERS WORK CLOSELY WITH GAFFNEY STAFF IN DESIGN AND SELECTIONS TO FIT THEIR FAMILY'S NEEDS AND DESIRES. THIS KITCHEN IS A STUNNING COMBINATION OF CUSTOM-BUILT CHERRY CABINETS, GRANITE COUNTERTOPS, ELEGANT LIGHTING AND CERAMIC TILE FLOOR.

USE OF LIGHT AND SPACE COMBINE TO BRING THE OUTDOOR ENTERTAINING AREAS INTO THE GREAT ROOM. THE STONE FIREPLACE AND HEARTH IS A WARM, INVITING GATHERING PLACE FOR FAMILY AND FRIENDS.

It's apparent the Gaffney team enjoys their work and their enthusiasm is reflected in everything they do. Staff members meet regularly with customers, discussing the progress of the work, making selections, and responding to customer concerns.

Gaffney Homes is known throughout the community for its outstanding quality, unquestioned integrity, and true professionalism. No one knows this better than the homeowners who have chosen this company to build their dream. Perhaps this is best summed up by Jeff and Sheila Davis:

"The Gaffney team has been interested in our input and emotion from the start. They are inventive, yet intent on quality and tradition of design. Scheduling was remarkably accurate—no surprises. With all questions raised, we received prompt and full attention. There is an obvious philosophy of incorporating our goals— even an appreciation of our observations, regardless of our inexperience. The entire staff recognizes the impact such a project has on a family and has shared a genuine excitement with us in this experience. This is truly a refined team of custom homebuilders—credible and trustworthy. Moreover, we have developed a friendship, which will certainly outlast the building process." ■

Gaffney's vision includes building Lifetime Communities, which he describes as: "communities that are so well designed and built that they are always a source of pleasure and pride for the inhabitants. Although people may move as circumstances dictate, the memories from this period will last a lifetime."

Gaffney is active in both local and national home-builder associations. As a Director of The National Association of Home Builders, he meets regularly with top builders from across the country. His openness in sharing ideas and his natural leadership abilities earned him a national reputation among his peers. In 1996, he was named one of the top 15 custom homebuilders in the country by *Custom Home Magazine.*

Gaffney Homes' customer service is legendary. The homeowner is treated as the most important member of a team of professionals that includes talented crafts-people, seasoned subcontractors, and reliable suppliers. Building this team is part of Mike Gaffney's vision. "We attract people who can see this vision and want to be a part in bringing it to reality."

GAFFNEY HOMES CREATES THE SPECIAL NICHES THAT ENHANCE THE LIVABILITY FOR EACH HOME. THIS LIBRARY PROVIDES A QUIET READING AREA FRAMED BY CHERRY BOOKSHELVES AND FRENCH DOORS.

R. D. WADE BUILDER, INC.

Randy Wade will be the first to admit that he got into the construction business quite by accident. In January 1960, Wade, a graduate of the University of Virginia, was lured away from a teaching career by a high school friend who encouraged him to join him in the building business. An entrepreneur at heart, Wade formed his own construction business in 1965. The company's defining moment came three years later when Wade began building multiple homes in the Canterbury Hills neighborhood. This experience led him to discover that volume building of semi-custom homes was the market niche for him.

A native of Charlottesville, Randy Wade appreciates the traditional roots of the area and his homes reflect that design. With over 2,600 homes built and a proven performance and sales record for nearly 40 years, R. D. Wade Builder is consistently chosen by prominent area developers to build in Charlottesville's premier locations. In 1988 Wade was selected as one of three primary builders to develop Forest Lakes and today is responsible for approximately one-third of all the homes built there. Wade has had entries in every annual Parade of Homes since its inception in the Charlottesville area, enabling potential buyers to view firsthand the quality of Wade-built homes.

"SCOTTISH HOME" IN GLENMORE OFFERS LUXURY LIVING WITH GROUND MAINTENANCE IN A COUNTRY CLUB COMMUNITY.

Wade currently builds in the communities of Redfields, Grayrock, Western Ridge, Forest Lakes, Still Meadows, and Glenmore with sales prices from $175,000 to $700,000 plus. In addition to building single-family homes, Wade was one of the earliest builders to enter the townhouse market and today develops sophisticated townhome communities with low-maintenance homes that appeal to a more active and secure lifestyle. Wade Homes is also active in the rental of townhomes and duplexes.

A family-run business that includes Wade's daughter Kelly and her husband Michael West, who is chief operating officer, R. D. Wade Builder has acquired an enviable reputation for building a well-designed home at a fair price and providing outstanding customer service after delivery. Integrity means a great deal to R. D. Wade, and the company prides itself on its responsiveness to the needs of the community. This is apparent in the company's impressive "on-time every-time" commitment to schedule. Wade attributes the company's enduring success to talented and dedicated employees and loyal subcontractors, many of whom have been associated with the company for over 30 years.

A respected name in the resale market with homes having a long-term value that is second to none, R. D. Wade Builders has securely established itself as one of the most successful and sought-after builders in the Charlottesville region. ■

STILL MEADOW HOME COMBINES EXTRA ATTENTION TO EXTERIOR MATERIALS AND DETAILS ALONG WITH FLEXIBLE INTERIOR LIVING SPACES.

MONTAGUE MILLER & CO. REALTORS

When Percy Montague III and the late Ben Miller founded Montague Miller & Co. Realtors in 1948, they envisioned it to be a family-run company that would be known for its integrity, professionalism,

COME AND ENJOY THE MOUNTAINS OF CENTRAL VIRGINIA ...
WE'LL SAVE YOU A SEAT!

and cohesiveness. Now over 50 years later, those three words continue to reflect the spirit and philosophy of the company.

Percy III and his son Percy IV, company CEO, President Carol Clarke, and Ben Miller's widow, still own Montague Miller, making it one of the oldest family-owned companies in the area. The company has a rich history, having developed many familiar Charlottesville neighborhoods, including Greenbriar, Woodbrook, Foxbrook, Redfields, and Millmont Street, which was named after Miller and Montague who developed most of the property behind Barracks Road. Another little known historical fact is that the Miller and Montague families assembled and still own the land at Fashion Square Mall which is on a 99-year land lease.

Thanks to its innovative marketing strategies, Montague Miller has become one of the top companies in Central Virginia with five locations, including offices in Charlottesville, Nelson, Orange, Fluvanna, and Madison Counties. The company handles everything from residential and commercial properties to new construction, land and lot sales, estate properties, and bed and breakfast inns.

Having one's family name attached to a business creates a high level of accountability that is pervasive throughout the company. The 60 plus agents who make up the Montague Miller team are professional, caring people who place a premium on developing client relationships by customizing every real estate transaction. They include many second and third generation realtors who enjoy serving the needs of several generations of customers and clients.

Being attuned to customer needs is something Montague Miller does well. When consumers indicated they preferred to have everything related to their real estate transaction under one roof—such as mortgage, closing, and home repair services—Montague Miller developed the first one-stop real estate service in the area. The Home Concierge service was another innovation. After clients kept turning to their agents for a recommendation of a handyman to do odd jobs around the house, Montague Miller created a database of licensed and bonded vendors. Now one call to the Home Concierge puts the public in touch with the professionals they need— from carpenters to plumbers to decorators and everything in between.

A proactive and cutting-edge company, Montague Miller has enjoyed many firsts in the local real estate market, including the first to use computers and the first to have a Web site. With a highly trained team of professionals who keep abreast of trends within the industry and the business community, Montague Miller remains one of the most dynamic, visionary, and innovative real estate companies in the market today. ■

PERCY MONTAGUE, IV, CHIEF EXECUTIVE OFFICER, AND CAROL F. CLARKE, PRESIDENT, MONTAGUE, MILLER & COMPANY REALTORS.

CHARLOTTESVILLE GLASS AND MIRROR CORPORATION

When John R. Corle began Charlottesville Glass and Mirror in 1954, he already had a wealth of knowledge about the glass business, having worked for Art Plate Glass in Baltimore, Maryland. In the beginning he was a one-man show, selling by day, cutting and installing glass at night. Soon the business became a family affair, with wife Doris handling bookkeeping

CHARLOTTESVILLE GLASS AND MIRROR CORPORATE HEADQUARTERS.

and the couple's children helping wherever they could. Dwight Corle remembers going to work with his dad from the age of ten. This early indoctrination led to a love for the business, and in 2000, Dwight purchased the company from his father.

Few companies know more about the glass business than Charlottesville Glass and Mirror. As the area's first and largest commercial and residential glass house, the company furnishes and installs everything from large storefront windows at shopping centers to glass for picture frames. Specialty items include Kawneer storefronts, replacement windows and doors, storm windows and doors, skylights, screen repair, auto glass, and custom work like artistically etched and beveled glass and mirrors. Charlottesville Glass and Mirror is the only glass shop within a 70-mile radius of Charlottesville that has its own beveling machine and skilled craftsmen who know how to use it, and can produce customized work in less than a week.

Examples of the company's workmanship include the glass at Scott Stadium, the University of Virginia Health Sciences Center, the Charlottesville-Albemarle Regional Airport, and the Northridge Building on 250 West. The company also is involved in historic restoration projects, including glasswork at Monticello and Michie Tavern. Corle, who works closely with area architects, also acts as a consultant to the Architectural Review Board to determine the appropriate use of glasswork in historical landmarks.

While other glass businesses in Charlottesville have changed ownership over the years, Charlottesville Glass and Mirror continues to be run by the Corle family. That kind of long-term commitment to the community has heightened customer confidence, earning the company a stellar reputation for producing a quality product at a good price, backed by unconditional customer satisfaction, personal service, and a qualified sales staff who does on-site estimates. Pick-up, delivery, and installation service are also available.

Will a third generation take over Charlottesville Glass and Mirror? Dwight Corle is hoping one if not all of his four children will become as passionate about glasswork as he was at an early age. It may only be a matter of time before the next generation steps forward to continue the pride of craftsmanship begun by John Corle nearly 50 years ago. ▪

COMPLETED GLASS PROJECT AT NORTHRIDGE OFFICE BUILDING.

PHOTO BY PHILIP BEAURLINE

PHOTO BY PHILIP BEAURLINE

UNIVERSITY OF VIRGINIA
■ ■ ■ ■ ■

"**N**obody can doubt my zeal for the general instruction of the people. Who first started that idea? I may surely say myself."
—*Thomas Jefferson*
Letter to General James Breckinridge, February 15, 1821

Thomas Jefferson had the vision; was the architect; lobbied for funding; supervised the construction; selected the faculty; and established the curriculum. And today, nearly two centuries after The University of Virginia opened its doors on March 7, 1825, the Jefferson mystique continues to permeate every part of the Academical Village. It's an almost mystical energy that descends over the Lawn, giving it that inexplicable sense of place, a feeling that Thomas Jefferson is still observing activities on the Grounds through his telescope atop Monticello. It is this indescribable sensation that sets U.Va. apart from other institutions and what ultimately compels people from all over the world to come—and for some to remain—in Charlottesville.

Jefferson considered the University of Virginia one of the greatest achievements of his life. In designing his Academical Village, he positioned the buildings so that students and faculty could live and learn together. At the heart of his design was a rectangular, grassy area known as The Lawn, flanked by student rooms and by 10 individually designed pavilions that housed faculty members and classrooms. Classes continue to be taught in two of those pavilions today.

At the end of the Lawn is the majestic Rotunda— Jefferson's "temple of knowledge"—that served as the University's original library and classroom building. The Rotunda's dome room still has the appearance of a library, with bookcases containing rare volumes cleverly hidden behind the room's columns. Its central space, filled with an effusion of light emanating from an oculus at the top of the dome, is used for meetings, student dinners, and special ceremonies.

In 2001, the University's enrollment was 18,550, representing all 50 states and 75 foreign countries. Although admission standards are highly competitive, the University strives for a diverse, well-rounded student body. Consequently, the criteria for accepting students are more than a high grade point average or SAT score. Evidence of good character, imagination, leadership, facility in self-expression, and dedication to service are also taken into consideration. Once an all-male school, the University began admitting women graduate students in 1920 and, starting in 1970, a limited number of women were admitted to the undergraduate College of Arts & Sciences. By 1972, the school was fully co-educational.

THE ROMAN PANTHEON SERVED AS THE MODEL FOR JEFFERSON'S DESIGN OF THE ROTUNDA, THE CENTERPIECE OF THE ACADEMICAL VILLAGE.

THE LAWN, ANCHORED AT ITS NORTH END BY THE ROTUNDA, STILL LOOKS MUCH AS IT DID IN JEFFERSON'S ERA.

The University of Virginia is the largest employer in the Charlottesville region. Of its nearly 12,000 employees, approximately half service the academic side and half the health sciences side. Nearly 2,000 full-time scholars comprise the University of Virginia's distinguished faculty. Selected from among the best in their respective fields, U.Va. faculty members not only teach, but also conduct groundbreaking research, publish books and journals, and more importantly, interact well with the student body.

U.S. News & World Report places many of the University's schools, departments, and programs among the nation's best. Of the University's 10 schools, five—including Architecture, Arts and Sciences, the McIntire School of Commerce, Engineering and Applied Sciences, and Nursing—offer both undergraduate and graduate studies. The Darden Graduate School of Business Administration, the School of Law, and the School of Medicine offer graduate studies. The Curry School of Education offers graduate degrees and a five-year dual degree program with the College of Arts and Sciences through which students receive both an undergraduate degree and a master's in teaching. The School of Continuing and Professional Studies offers a part-time undergraduate degree and many other programs and graduate study.

U.Va.'s vast library system is ranked in the top 25 in the country. Its 14 libraries contain four million volumes, supplemented by one of the world's largest electronic text libraries, and a valuable collection of rare books and manuscripts. The library participates in an inter-library loan program, enabling Virginia residents to share in its resources.

The University's athletics program—consisting of 12 men's and 12 women's intercollegiate sports—is part of the highly competitive Atlantic Coast Conference. The Sears Directors' Cup, which ranks the overall success of Division I athletic programs in up to 20 sports, placed U.Va. 13th in the nation in the final 1999-2000 standings.

The University recently completed a $1.4 billion capital campaign to support building projects, scholarships, fellowships, faculty salaries, and academic programs. This ambitious undertaking has added to the University's stabilizing impact on the region's economy. In addition, U.Va.'s research enterprise is growing at a phenomenal rate. Research parks and incentives are attracting new and environmentally friendly businesses to the area. It is estimated that for every million dollars in research money, 32 jobs are created directly or indirectly through services within the community. In addition, the University partners with many local civic organizations, the community college, and area businesses to provide opportunities and address issues of concern to all such as jobs, controlled growth, and transportation.

The University of Virginia consistently has been named among the top schools in the country by national magazines and organizations. In September 2001, *U.S. News & World Report* ranked U.Va. the nation's number two public university and 21st among all national universities.

STUDENTS CONSIDER IT AN HONOR TO LIVE IN ONE OF THE PRESTIGIOUS LAWN ROOMS AT THE UNIVERSITY.

PATIENTS ARRIVE AT THE 560-BED UNIVERSITY HOSPITAL FROM ACROSS THE NATION AND FROM AROUND THE WORLD. A TEACHING HOSPITAL AND THE CENTERPIECE OF THE U.VA. HEALTH SYSTEM, IT HAS BEEN CONSISTENTLY RANKED AMONG THE 100 BEST HOSPITALS IN THE COUNTRY. UNIVERSITY HOSPITAL IS ALSO A LEVEL 1 TRAUMA CENTER FOR CENTRAL VIRGINIA.

University of Virginia Health System

As with the academic side, the University of Virginia Health System has achieved a high ranking among hospitals nationwide. It has been named among the 100 Top Hospitals in the country for three years in a row by Solucient and since 1989 has been recognized by *U.S. News & World Report* as one of America's Best Hospitals. This fact has not been lost on the area's burgeoning senior community who choose to retire in the Charlottesville region in part because of the accessibility of quality health care.

Because of its affiliation with a nationally acclaimed university, the Health System attracts world-class physicians and staff who are interested in learning and are drawn to a medical facility that provides innovative care. Being situated in an area known for its exceptional beauty is also a plus, for it gives health-care professionals an opportunity to enjoy a rural lifestyle while practicing the kind of sophisticated medicine that's normally associated with a more urban environment.

The U.Va. Health System has evolved into a world-class medical facility known for its exceptional primary care and specialty services. The medical center encompasses a 560-bed hospital, numerous clinics on the U.Va. campus and at over 40 locations throughout Charlottesville and neighboring counties, a network of almost 600 physicians, an extensive library, and outstanding medical and nursing schools.

Now entering its second century of care, the Health System remains one of the most innovative health-care facilities in the country. Because it is a teaching hospital, patients are assured that any physician they see represents a depth of expertise. The Health System offers specialized care and outstanding physicians who offer coordinated treatment through centers focused in specific areas, including:

- The Cancer Center: Providing the most advanced treatment available for all types of cancer and access to a wide range of experimental drugs offered through its clinical trials program.
- The Heart Center: Offering prevention, diagnosis, drug therapies, surgery, transplant, and rehabilitation services.
- The Digestive Health Center: Treating all types of gastrointestinal diseases.
- The Neurosciences Service Center: Caring for victims of stroke, epilepsy, degenerative diseases, brain tumors, neonatal, and developmental disorders.
- The Women's Place: Addressing health concerns affecting women at every stage of life.
- The Children's Medical Center: Dedicated to the care of children from birth through adolescence.

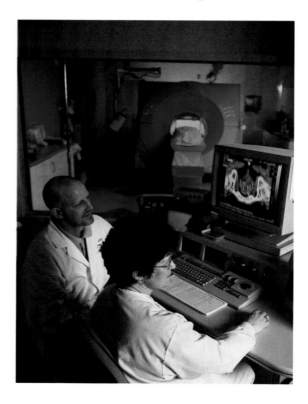

THE RIGHT IMAGE IS CRITICAL. THE U.VA. HEALTH SYSTEM IS A LEADER AMONG INSTITUTIONS DEVELOPING STATE-OF-THE-ART MEDICAL IMAGING TECHNOLOGIES, SUCH AS ULTRASOUND, MAGNETIC RESONANCE IMAGING, DIGITAL MAMMOGRAPHY, AND ELECTROMECHANICAL MAPPING.

- The Center for Adult Rehabilitation and Elder Care (CARE): Providing professionals trained in geriatric health care.
- Level 1 Trauma Center: An exemplary emergency department that treats all types of medical emergencies and features air ambulance service and a chest pain center for the rapid diagnosis of heart problems.

These centers all interact with each other, resulting in a true collaboration that gives patients the assurance that an optimal treatment plan is prescribed for their care.

Each year, the nation's most promising medical students enroll in the University of Virginia School of Medicine, attracted in part by the fact that the school has one of the most prominent medical faculties in the country. Like the School of Medicine, the University of Virginia School of Nursing enjoys a national reputation for excellence in education, research, and practice and is ranked among the top 25 public nursing schools in the country.

The Health System's extensive research program enables patients to participate in clinical trials and have access to medical technology in its development stage, while its library provides up-to-date information and research findings to health-care professionals

FROM PEDIATRICS TO GERIATRICS, TOP-FLIGHT HEALTH CARE FOR EVERY STAGE OF LIFE IS AVAILABLE AT THE U.VA. HEALTH SYSTEM. BACKED BY THE RESOURCES OF THE HEALTH SYSTEM AND A NETWORK OF NEARLY 600 PHYSICIANS, U.VA. PROVIDES NOT ONLY THE LATEST IN MEDICAL TECHNOLOGIES BUT COMPASSIONATE, PATIENT-FOCUSED HEALTH CARE AT ITS BEST.

throughout the area. This commitment to excellence also extends to the health-care needs of the community. U.Va. residents volunteer their services in free clinics throughout the area, while the nursing school offers clinical services at some of the local housing projects. The hospital's outreach program is extensive, sponsoring health education, information services, and classes; support groups; low-cost mammograms; free skin, ear/nose/throat, and prostate cancer screenings; and screenings for anxiety and depression.

The Health System's full-time and volunteer staff, coupled with a network of support staff including chaplains and social workers, are known for their caring, warmth, compassion, and genuine concern for the patient's physical and emotional well-being. These dedicated men and women, combined with medical technology and practices that are superior to most, are why the University of Virginia Health System is considered one of the most cutting-edge medical facilities in the world.

Thomas Jefferson believed the role of education was to prepare citizens to make responsible decisions as part of living in a democracy. That is still the focus at the University of Virginia. Jefferson's ideas on education and democracy are consciously attended to and are built not only into the school's academic life but in its social fabric as well. In that regard, the legacy of Thomas Jefferson's philosophy continues to be played out as vigorously in the 21st century as it did when it was founded two centuries ago. ■

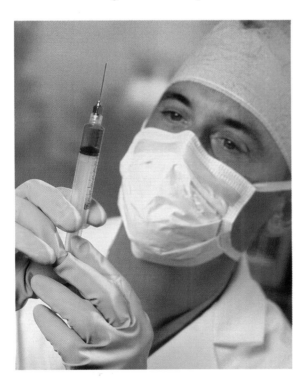

WHETHER IT'S PRIMARY CARE OR THE SERVICES OF A TOP SPECIALIST, THE U.VA. HEALTH SYSTEM'S PATIENTS CAN QUICKLY BENEFIT FROM THE RESULTS OF SOME OF THE MOST ADVANCED MEDICAL RESEARCH BEING CONDUCTED ANYWHERE IN THE WORLD TODAY.

ST. ANNE'S-BELFIELD SCHOOL

St. Anne's-Belfield School is one of Charlottesville's oldest and most prestigious private schools. Located near the University of Virginia on two campuses that total almost 50 acres, St. Anne's-Belfield is a coeducational, college-preparatory day school for approximately 825 students in pre-school through grade 12. The school also offers a five-day and a seven-day boarding school program for students in grades 9 through 12.

ST. ANNE'S FIRST GRADUATING CLASS IN 1913.

St. Anne's-Belfield School has a rich heritage dating back to 1856 with the opening of The Albemarle Female Institute. In 1910, Reverend Henry B. Lee, Rector of Christ Episcopal Church, spearheaded the purchase of the institute and reopened it as St. Anne's School. The following year, Nancy Gordon opened The Blue Ridge Primary School, later known as Stonefield. After Gordon's death, Stonefield merged with the University Country Day School (the Bellair School) to become Belfield. In 1975, Belfield joined with St. Anne's to create a legacy of high academic standards and an enduring tradition that enriches the lives of St. Anne's-Belfield students today.

Renowned for its strong academic orientation, St. Anne's-Belfield's primary goal is to provide students with a solid preparation for college with concern for the individual both as a student and as a person. To accomplish this, the school's faculty is carefully selected not only for their scholarly commitment

(71 percent of the upper school faculty hold graduate degrees), but for their enthusiasm and willingness to view themselves both as counselors as well as teachers. Students and faculty at St. Anne's-Belfield enjoy a very special relationship that is rare in other academic institutions. A mutual respect exists between students and teachers, with an open-door policy that encourages communication and total accessibility. Faculty members, many of whom have been teaching at the school for years, are not only dedicated to the students, but they have a strong emotional tie to the school as an institution. This level of commitment perpetuates a family atmosphere within the school. Class sizes remain small with an average of 15 students per class. This dedication to individual learning is a highly successful formula, considering the school's impressive academic scores. The median SAT I score for the class of 2000, for instance, was 1290.

Just as the faculty is carefully chosen, so, too, are the students. In an individualized admission process, the school looks for inquisitive, enthusiastic, and conscientious students who will bring their own special talents, energy, and skills to the school community. St. Anne's-Belfield seeks to enroll students who possess the motivation and intelligence to meet the school's academic requirements, who are committed to their academic, personal, and social growth, who exhibit personal integrity, show respect and concern for others, and who demonstrate curiosity and a passion for learning.

In keeping with the school's philosophy to nurture body, mind, and spirit, St. Anne's-Belfield has an inter-scholastic athletic program that has brought home countless championship trophies. The philosophy of the athletic program stresses participation, regardless

RANDOLPH HALL, THE UPPER SCHOOL
ACADEMIC BUILDING.

of a student's previous experience or level of talent. Most coaches are teachers who instill in students the desire to be winners at life as opposed to winning the game. Every student is encouraged to participate in the interscholastic program during at least one season per year resulting in more than an 85 percent participation rate in team sports.

Academic and athletic opportunities aside, St. Anne's-Belfield is also known for its long-standing traditions. Nowhere is that more apparent than in the chapel program and the honor code. Although St. Anne's-Belfield is firmly committed to providing a nondenominational, nonsectarian environment for its students, weekly chapel services are a pivotal part of the St. Anne's-Belfield experience. Emphasizing values rather than theology, chapel services give students a time of inner reflection that is so essential in nurturing the soul.

Another of the school's traditions—the honor code—has been refined over the years, but its basic premise—"a student is not to lie, cheat, or steal"—fosters an environment in which honorable behavior is encouraged, nurtured, and is the standard for all conduct. At St. Anne's-Belfield, there are no locks on lockers and responsibility for honesty is placed squarely on the shoulders of the student.

From the Civil War until now, St. Anne's-Belfield has retained its character, keeping pace with the times without sacrificing the integrity of the school. With a strong and stable leadership, coupled with supportive parents, St. Anne's-Belfield continues to fulfill the school's philosophy to "create a challenging yet charitable

LACROSSE IS A POPULAR SPRING SPORT FOR BOYS AND GIRLS.

atmosphere where students gain skills necessary for both creative and disciplined thought, where they have opportunities to achieve in athletic and artistic endeavors, where they understand their responsibility as members of a community, and where high expectations for both their personal and intellectual lives are complemented by the school's commitment to nurturing students in the spiritual dimension of life." ■

SMALL CLASS SIZE PROMOTES CLOSE INTERACTION BETWEEN STUDENTS AND TEACHERS.

FEDERAL EXECUTIVE INSTITUTE

For years, the Federal Executive Institute (FEI) has been an object of curiosity in the Charlottesville community. The truth is, the FEI was established by Presidential Order in 1968 to provide leadership training and development for the top echelon of government, the Senior Executive Service. As part of the U.S. Office of Personnel Management, FEI hosts executives from more than 80 U.S. domestic and defense agencies as well as several international governments who participate in programs designed to enhance their leadership skills.

Located on 14 acres off Emmet Street in what was formerly The Thomas Jefferson Inn, FEI added buildings to the property in 1989 and 1998. Executives who come to FEI stay in comfortable, private rooms furnished with up-to-date books on leadership and results management to support them in their "round-the-clock" reading and class preparation. Seminars and workshops are conducted in well-equipped, on-site classrooms. Courses regarding policy making in the Constitutional system, global perspectives and public action, personal leadership in government, and transforming public organizations are led by FEI's full-time and adjunct faculty. The program is holistic by design and includes physical fitness activities and well-prepared, health conscious meals to address the total person.

PAMELA B. GWIN HALL IS THE NEWEST OF FEI'S BUILDINGS. IT WAS COMPLETED IN 1998.

During their first week, executives undergo a battery of assessments. After studying feedback from these assessments, participants select courses that would best enrich their particular leadership skills. These courses may focus on a range of competencies and are designed to help executives develop an understanding of and appreciation for the political, social, economic, environmental, and cultural conditions in which they work. But FEI provides something else—a no-threat environment where people are free to explore who they are, where they want to go, and how to get there. The result is dramatic. People leave FEI saying the experience has changed their lives—so much so that after graduation many continue to remain active in FEI's vibrant alumni association.

FEI and its enrollees contribute to the Charlottesville community in numerous ways: patronizing local hotels, restaurants, entertainment, shopping, and historic attractions. In addition, each class forms a Community Committee that donates a monetary gift on behalf of the entire class to a local charity, government, or service group.

Of its many achievements, FEI's greatest accomplishment may be its longevity. FEI has maintained a non-partisan atmosphere in which healthy, open, honest dialogue is encouraged. For over 32 years, the Federal Executive Institute has remained committed to its mission—"great leaders for great government"—and to fulfilling the original Presidential mandate to "improve the quality of government for the American people." ■

FEI'S MAIN ENTRANCE HAS WELCOMED EXECUTIVES TO THEIR "HOME AWAY FROM HOME" FOR LEADERSHIP TRAINING AND DEVELOPMENT SINCE 1968.

TANDEM FRIENDS SCHOOL
■ ■ ■ ■ ■

When John Howard and Duncan Alling founded Tandem School in 1970, they wanted to create a school that would foster wisdom, kindness, and the ability to balance freedom and responsibility. They believed in giving students more power and more voice within the guiding principles of academic excellence and moral responsibility, thus producing conscientious individuals who think and act independently and creatively.

Recognizing that Tandem shared many of the same values as Quaker schools, i.e., a tradition of personal and intellectual integrity, honoring each person, nurturing individual talents, and developing ethical values and social responsibility—Tandem became affiliated with the Friends Council on Education (Quaker) and became Tandem Friends School in 1995.

Tandem is home to 215-plus students in grades 5 through 12 who receive an education in which intellectual, ethical, artistic, and athletic ideals are pursued. Because enrollment is limited, Tandem selects students who value a spiritual, egalitarian, kind, and creative community; thrive on independent, imaginative thought; are fully engaged in learning; and seek the best from themselves and their community. Operating out of mutual respect and in keeping with a 300-year-old Quaker practice, students and teachers address each other by their first name. Small class sizes encourage a written and verbal dialogue that results in students who are sophisticated scholars, powerful thinkers, and critical questioners.

Tandem Friends School has an outstanding college preparatory program and students traditionally do well in college admissions. A program unique to Tandem that has been acclaimed by college admissions offices is The Senior Project. This yearlong ungraded project encourages seniors to find a mentor and learn to do something they always wanted to do—from building a canoe, to starting a small business, to skydiving.

Because Tandem students are taught to value themselves and the role they play in the community, they are required to participate in community service activities both on and off campus. As a result, graduates have developed habits of social responsibility and ethical conduct. They leave Tandem knowing they have the ability to create positive change in the communities they join.

Ever mindful of the Quaker philosophy of honoring and nurturing the Light within everyone, Tandem's faculty is dedicated to the intellectual, spiritual, and moral growth of each student as a unique and valued individual. At Tandem Friends School, faculty and staff see the grand potential within every child, and seek to create and maintain a challenging, engaging, supportive, and secure environment in which to learn and grow. ■

CHURCH OF THE INCARNATION
■ ■ ■ ■ ■

The Church of the Incarnation, a Roman Catholic parish founded in 1976, is a community of Christians striving to live the gospel of Jesus Christ in their daily lives. Comprised of over 1,000 families, the parish encourages parishioners to become actively involved in worship, religious education, youth ministry, community life, and social justice projects.

The heart of the parish is the gathering of members in the Worship Center, a space designed to enhance the communal aspect of Christian worship. Visitors to the parish are warmly welcomed and truly made to feel at home regardless of where they are in their spiritual journey. That sense of belonging is what draws people to Incarnation from across the Charlottesville region. For parishioners, however, extending a warm welcome is the fulfillment of Christ's message. At Incarnation, people receive the love of Christ and in turn share that love with others.

INCARNATION PARISHIONERS ASSIST IN SORTING AND PACKING FOOD FOR THE ANNUAL CHRISTMAS DISTRIBUTION TO THE NEEDY.

Believing that faith should be extended beyond the walls of the church, the parish sponsors local and international service ministries. Incarnation provides an Outreach Ministry to families in need of food, emergency financial assistance, budget planning, and supportive counseling. Incarnation sponsors health, education, and economic development projects in rural Haiti as well. The parish also supports local and international efforts for social change to eliminate the root causes of poverty and injustice.

In addition to its outreach to others, the parish realizes that it starts within. The liturgies and sacraments incorporate beautiful music and are well celebrated; children and youth are provided ample opportunities to grow through religious education and service projects; and the parish provides social opportunities for parishioners and guests to enjoy fellowship.

As varied as the ministries, services, and socials are, Incarnation recognizes the need to improve upon what it has built. The future will bring renewed emphasis in the form of retreats and Christian adult education classes. Other areas of focus will emphasize meeting the spiritual needs of the growing Hispanic community, guiding non-traditional families, improving communication within the parish, and focusing upon its welcoming of new parishioners.

The Church of the Incarnation desires to support and continue its long-held traditions of dynamic and prayerful liturgies, outreach to those less fortunate, involvement of youth at all levels, a welcoming and inclusive attitude, and recognition that its members are called not just to see Christ in others but to be Christ to others as well.

After 25 years of faithful service, the Church of the Incarnation is poised to deepen its prayer life and social ministries to continue being a strong, spirit-filled community in the Charlottesville region and beyond. ■

PHOTO BY PHILIP BEAURLINE

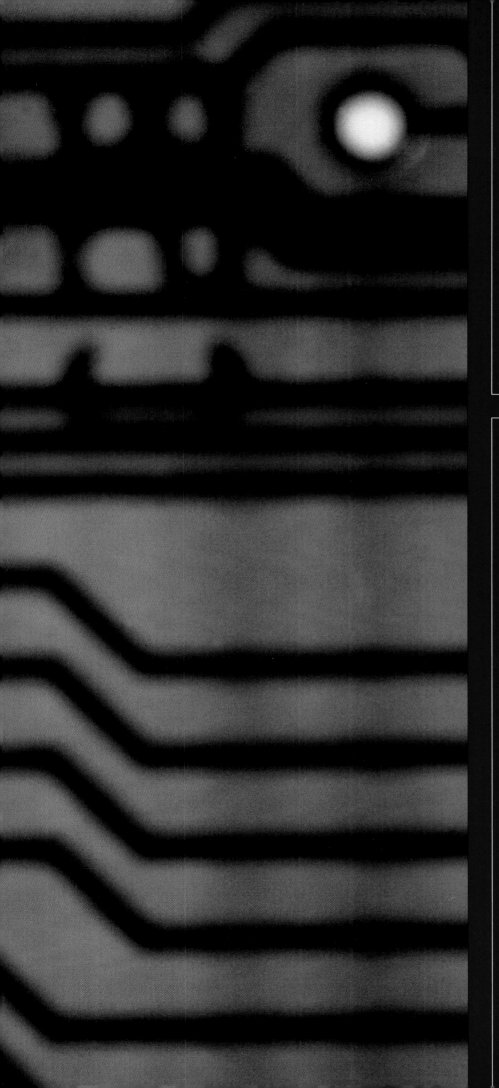

11 | **CHAPTER ELEVEN**

MANUFACTURING, DISTRIBUTION & TECHNOLOGY

. . . . .

PHOTO © MICHAEL P. MANHEIM

SPRINT
■ ■ ■ ■ ■

Nearly everyone knows Sprint as the premier provider of local and long-distance telephone service in the Charlottesville region, but this 100-plus-year-old company does so much more, with a sophisticated menu of services and products that have made Sprint the standard by which other telephone companies are measured.

While Sprint services the telecommunications needs of the Charlottesville area, it is in fact a global communications company, a leader in integrating diverse technologies, and is one of the world's largest carriers of Internet traffic. The company built and operates the United States' first nationwide, all-digital, fiber-optic network and provides a portfolio of advanced data communications services.

Because of its deployment of digital equipment and fiber optics, Sprint has been able to offer Charlottesville business and residential customers a choice of state-of-art products and services that are ahead of many telephone companies, including those serving much larger areas. In 1999, Charlottesville became the first Sprint local operating area to experience FastConnect, Sprint's digital subscriber line, offering high-speed Internet access on a large scale in the Charlottesville area.

Sprint employs more than 450 people in its Charlottesville-area offices, including customer service personnel, installers, and support staff who service subscribers in the city of Charlottesville, and counties of Albemarle, Fluvanna, and Greene. As part of Sprint's worldwide organization of some 80,000 people, local employees take pride in the fact that they're a part of a cutting-edge company that takes care of its own.

When people think of what a local telephone company means to their community, they think of

SERVICE TECH CHECKING PAIR IN PEDESTAL.

service and accessibility. Whether a subscriber is a family living on a remote mountaintop, or a business in the center of town, Sprint provides the same level of quality service to the average residential customer as it does to large corporations in a cost-effective, cost-efficient manner.

In the Charlottesville area, Sprint customers can select from a wide variety of innovative services such as Caller ID, Repeat Dialing, Call Waiting, Sprint Personal Messenger, and others, and they can combine the features in popular Sprint Solutions bundles with local and long-distance calling plans, all for one low price. Business customers can enjoy Centrex services, as well as high-speed data options through services like T1 lines, asynchronous transfer mode (ATM), and frame relay. ISDN and in-state calling rates are among the lowest anywhere, and Sprint also provides 90-megabit-per-second service for Internet backbone traffic. Sprint's FastConnect DSL offers dedicated high-speed Internet access for residential and business customers without the bandwidth dilution problems associated with cable DSL.

SPRINT STORE MANAGER AND TEAM IN FRONT OF RETAIL
STORE IN SEMINOLE SQUARE SHOPPING CENTER LOCATED IN
CHARLOTTESVILLE, VIRGINIA.

CUSTOMER CARE REPRESENTATIVE LOCATED IN CHARLOTTESVILLE, VIRGINIA WORKING WITH CUSTOMERS.

Since its 1993 merger with Centel Corp., Sprint has maintained a significant presence in the community. Sprint and its employees have strengthened their leadership role in economic development and community involvement throughout the region. Each day the public affairs office screens requests for contributions and company involvement in any number of worthy causes. To keep abreast of community needs, Sprint's local public affairs manager, Jim Harlow, is an active member of numerous public boards, civic groups, and clubs.

Sprint may not have a monopoly on the telecommunications business in Charlottesville, but the company and its people believe that having competition has provided the company with new growth opportunities. Challenged by the ever-evolving communications business, Sprint continues to develop innovative products and services to maintain its position as a leading provider of communications solutions for business, commercial, educational, and residential customers in the world. ■

Sprint's commitment to the Charlottesville region is enormous. The company has invested millions of dollars in network infrastructure in facilities, in economic development efforts, and contributions to the community. In 2001, Sprint expects to spend more than $10.8 million on Charlottesville-area projects and more than $65 million statewide to maintain and improve service in its local service area, including expenditures for fiber-optic connectivity, network redundancy, and service enhancements.

Sprint's network integrity and infrastructure quality has made the Charlottesville region a fiber-rich, robust network that acts as a location magnet to new businesses that are high-end communications users. Sprint's central offices are connected by fiber-optic cable and numerous survivable fiber "rings" that help support network integrity and decrease the risk of widespread outages that could be caused by cut cables. The ring architecture provides route diversity, another factor that increases the region's attractiveness to high-volume data users.

Because the Charlottesville region is a main focus for Sprint, the company works closely with economic development agencies across the area to project the growth of any given area and then stay ahead of demand by planning for construction projects that allow for expansion. These projects result in a sizable investment that Sprint makes in the community because the taxes it pays on these capital investments ultimately go to benefit schools, police, and fire protection. In 2000 alone, Sprint paid more than $3.8 million in county, city, and town taxes statewide, including some $537,000 to Charlottesville and about $431,000 to Albemarle County.

LOCAL SPRINT MANAGEMENT TEAM AT SPRINT BUILDING IN CHARLOTTESVILLE, VIRGINIA. LEFT TO RIGHT: BARRY PENDELTON, MARGARET WRIGHT, PHILLIP CASHWELL, LARRY KIRBY, LINDA VIAR, JIM HARLOW.

BIOTAGE, INC. A DYAX CORP. COMPANY

■ ■ ■ ■ ■

Looking at Biotage now, it is hard to believe that a little over 10 years ago the company operated on a shoestring budget out of someone's garage. Today, with over 125 employees and anticipated sales of $20 million in 2001, Biotage has become a preferred supplier of purification-separation systems and consumables for the pharmaceutical, biopharmaceutical, and specialty chemical industries.

BIOTAGE PRODUCES PREPACKED CARTRIDGES AND SYSTEMS FOR FASTER, SAFER, AND EASIER PHARMACEUTICAL COMPOUND PURIFICATION.

Biotage was founded in 1989 and became a purification and separations product company owned by Dyax Corp. Dyax Corp develops and commercializes new technologies for the pharmaceutical and biopharmaceutical industries in addition to discovering new therapeutic compounds. Company founders, Henry Blair and Sheridan (Sherry) Snyder had previously founded Genzyme, one of the world's largest and most profitable biotech companies.

Although Biotage came from an impressive lineage, it took nearly six years before the company discovered a novel way to purify pharmaceutical drugs faster, safer, and easier than any other previous technique. That discovery changed Biotage's future. Sales began to soar, and by August 2000, Dyax Corp., and hence Biotage, Inc., executed a highly successful Initial Public Offering. This allowed the company to raise sufficient capital to fund its growth for the future.

Known for having technically innovative products, Biotage has the distinction of being the only company in its field that can follow a drug from the time it is discovered by the chemist, through clinical trials, and then purify it on very large scale for mass production. In fact, Biotage maintains a market and technical leadership position for its Drug Discovery bench purification

therapeutic proteins and antibodies. In 2001, 80 percent of the company's sales were from products that have been on the market for four years or less.

To keep pace with its rapid growth, Biotage has plans to move into a new 50,000-square-foot facility to house production space, offices, and state-of-the-art laboratories for product and chemistry development. The building has the capability of expanding to 85,000 square feet to accommodate the company's projected growth to 350 employees and sales of $50 plus million by 2007.

Much if not all of Biotage's success is due to its employees. The corporate philosophy is based on the idea that the employees are the company. Besides acknowledging the value of what each Biotage employee offers, this belief has also helped the company to maintain its position of leadership in the marketplace. The Charlottesville region has proven to be fertile ground for recruiting Biotage employees. The company seeks to hire the most qualified, talented, and energetic people and employs numerous research chemists as well as mechanical and electrical engineers. A number of employees are University of Virginia graduates. On those occasions when the company conducts a national search, having the corporate headquarters in Charlottesville is an advantage in luring the brightest and best talent to the area. In addition to its corporate headquarters, Biotage maintains subsidiary offices in England and Japan and is planning to locate additional offices in Germany, Switzerland, and Italy in the near future.

DAVE B. PATTESON IS PRESIDENT AND CEO OF BIOTAGE, INC., A DYAX CORP. COMPANY.

Biotage employees enjoy a benefits package that gives them a sense of ownership in the company. Every employee owns stock in the company and works in an informal environment where voicing opinions is encouraged. Staff meetings to discuss tactics and strategy are held often while monthly full-company employee meetings provide a forum to discuss issues and keep abreast of the company's goals. Department heads are encouraged to take their staff off-site periodically for fun and relaxation. These types of activities keep moral high and turnover low.

Biotage researchers maintain a mutually beneficial relationship with researchers at the University who are experts in the field of pharmaceutical chemistry and proteins. Since the human genome was sequenced last year, scientists have been working on determining how the genes express themselves in both a disease and in a healthy condition in a human cell format. This information will enable researchers to identify which new target drugs need to be developed. Until recently only 400 to

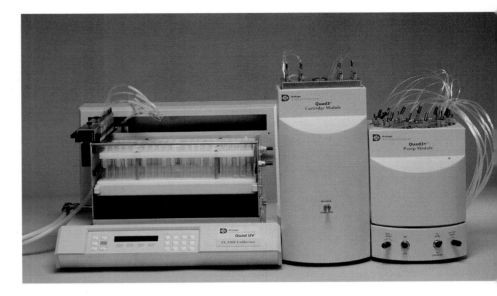

THE BIOTAGE QUAD3+™ PARALLEL FLASH PURIFICATION™ SYSTEM ALLOWS CHEMISTS TO INCREASE THEIR PURIFICATION OF ORGANIC COMPOUNDS WITH UNEQUAL SIMPLICITY.

500 known disease targets for drugs had been identified. Now that the human genome has been sequenced, it is estimated that a minimum of 10,000 new targets will be identified within the next 10 years.

The movement from a sequenced human genome to functional genomics and proteomics has created additional opportunities for Biotage. The effort required to purify, enhance, and screen these proteome permutations is immense. Biotage intends to apply its systems, disposable columns, automation, and system integration expertise to this rapidly emerging market.

Other researchers at the University of Virginia are well-known experts in the field of protein chemistry and cellular level bio-activity. Biotage develops and provides systems to speed up the process of purifying those complex matrixes. Already the company has taken a two-day process and reduced it to 20 minutes. That turnaround time is expected to be further reduced, thus enabling chemists to have a higher productivity rate and increase the number of potential drug leads making it through pharmaceutical companies. For the average consumer this means that new drugs will make it to the marketplace sooner—and that's good for everyone.

From its humble beginnings in a garage environment to the multi-million-dollar company it is today, Biotage continues to break ground in developing innovative products and systems whose impact reaches around the globe. ∎

THE BIOTAGE MISSION IS TO BE THE PREFERRED SUPPLIER OF PURIFICATION-SEPARATION SYSTEMS AND CONSUMABLES FOR THE PHARMACEUTICAL, BIO-PHARMACEUTICAL, AND SPECIALTY CHEMICAL INDUSTRIES.

MICROAIRE SURGICAL INSTRUMENTS
■ ■ ■ ■ ■

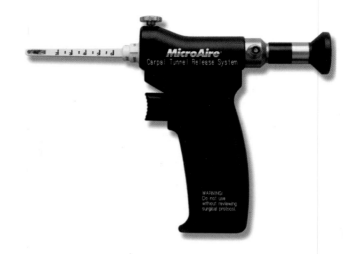

Orthopedic surgeons are the craftsmen of the human skeleton. They are exceptionally talented at their craft, but to create a true masterpiece, they need the proper tools. MicroAire Surgical Instruments—one of the country's foremost suppliers of high-quality precision instruments for orthopedic surgery—gives them those tools.

MicroAire began in California as the Health Care Division of American Safety Equipment Corporation. In 1977, it produced its first three instruments that featured a pencil grip style and fingertip lever. The Marmon Group acquired the company the following year and continued developing innovative products to give surgeons finer control when operating on small bones such as those found in the ankle, hand, and face. MicroAire was and continues to be an innovative force in the industry. During the early '80s, the company introduced sterile-packaged disposable saw blades, drills, and burs. MicroAire soared to the next level by successfully marketing these products at a much fairer price than its competition and before long achieved a secure position in the marketplace.

The company decided to move from Valencia, California, to Charlottesville, Virginia, partly in response to the University of Virginia's recruitment of companies like MicroAire for its North Fork Research Park. The company broke ground in February 1995 and moved into its new 45,000-square-foot facility in the fall of that same year.

Moving across country created a challenge for MicroAire. Not only was it disruptive, but it came at a time when the industry as a whole was going through some drastic changes. MicroAire's first two years in Charlottesville were difficult. Of the 90 people who worked for the company in California, only about 24 agreed to move and less than half of those stayed. Besides staffing considerations, the company had been concerned about transportation and shipping issues, wondering if the move from a suburb of Los Angeles to a more rural area in Virginia would be a challenge. Fortunately, the move to the Charlottesville region proved an advantageous one. The close proximity of the Charlottesville-Albemarle Airport with its connections through Charlotte, Cincinnati, La Guardia, Pittsburgh, Philadelphia, and Washington D.C. alleviated the company's concerns about the ease of getting products and people to other destinations. The company also found the Charlottesville region produced a reliable, easily trained employee base with a good work ethic. Another plus was the presence of the University of Virginia and its orthopedics lab that the company used for a number of research projects. MicroAire also tapped into U.Va.'s graduate pool, successfully recruiting a number of interns from the school, including mechanical engineers right out of the master's program.

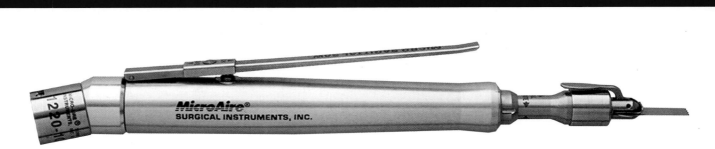

The company's product line design, assembly, packaging, and testing are done in Virginia. All finished goods are warehoused in Charlottesville and shipped to customers throughout the world. MicroAire has 100 plus representatives that sell over 3,500 catalogue products throughout the United States and representation in 50 countries around the world. With 110 Charlottesville-based employees, the company is twice the size today as it was when it came to Virginia in 1995. Employees enjoy attractive wages and benefits, and a comprehensive training program, making MicroAire one of the most desirable employers in the area.

MicroAire instruments are of superior quality with more power, precision control, and flexibility than similar instruments on the market today. The company competes with major companies in the orthopedic arena for the orthopedic bone cutting instrument business, but feels its high quality design, production standards, innovative product line, and fair pricing give the company its competitive edge.

It's apparent MicroAire has done all the right things when it comes to bone cutting, so it's no wonder it has such an optimistic view of the future. The company continues to look for acquisitions and is developing a new Web site to enable customers to transact orders over the Internet. Job growth is anticipated to continue and within five years the company hopes to expand by building on the vacant property reserved next to its current location.

Fran Lavin, MicroAire's president since 1994, is the first to admit that providing high-quality instruments for bone surgery is not a glamorous business, but considering that orthopedic surgeons around the world have come to rely on MicroAire's precision tools, it is a business that is cutting edge when it comes to the small bone surgical market. ∎

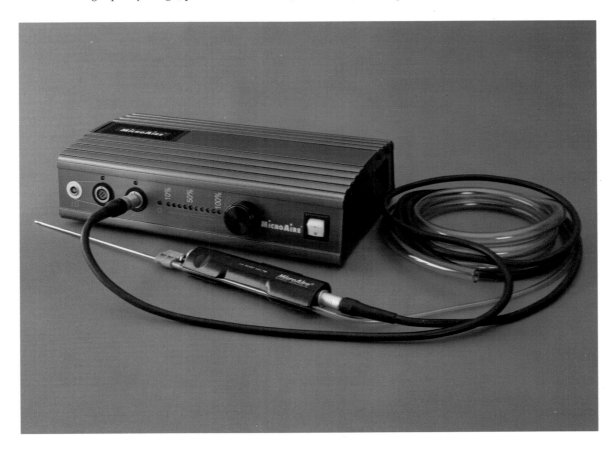

TECHNICOLOR
▪ ▪ ▪ ▪ ▪

Not many people in the Charlottesville region realize that the DVDs they rent or buy are actually made right here. Technicolor, the world's leading video-cassette, CD-ROM, CD-Audio, and DVD manufacturing company has been operating since 1986. It is one of the area's fastest growing private companies with 715 permanent employees.

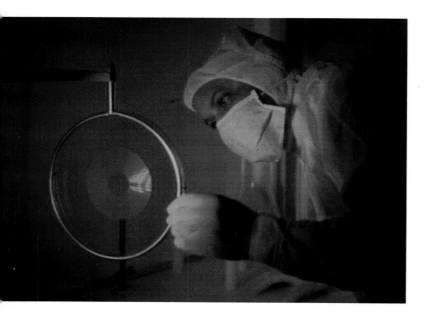

THE PRELIMINARY PROCESS OF MASTERING THE DATA FOR MASS REPLICATION OF CDS IS CRITICAL.

How this Welsh-originated manufacturer came to settle in Greene County is a tale worth telling. The company was founded in 1958 by Count Alexander Numa Labinski, a Polish opera singer living in Wales who had a penchant for quality. Nabinski created Nimbus Records, Ltd., as a private recording company and record label to preserve the performance of great classical artists utilizing leading-edge recording technology to reproduce concert-hall quality sound.

Over the years, the company never lost its technological edge. In early 1982, Nimbus obtained a license to manufacture compact discs (CDs) and with the help of Dr. Jonathan Halliday, designed and produced its own system for manufacturing CDs. In less than a year, Nimbus successfully completed the development of its own proprietary CD laser mastering system, "the Nimbus-Halliday Laser Mastering System," which to this day sets the industry standard for CD mastering performance.

Nimbus was one of the first companies to digitally record music on CDs, and after establishing itself as a world-class audio CD manufacturer, the company recognized the potential of CD-ROM technology. Desiring to capitalize on the American market, the company built a 43,000-square-foot production facility in Ruckersville.

Why Ruckersville? The story is told that Nabinski had a vision of rolling hills much like his home in Monmouth, Wales. Whether Greene County matched the Count's vision or if it was simply a matter of economics, the company purchased a 250-acre tract of land west of Route 29 and 10 minutes north of the Charlottesville-Albemarle Airport. The plant began production in 1986 and today, after two expansions, has grown to a 117,000-square-foot facility. In addition, a 311,000-square-foot building is leased for packaging purposes.

The property contains a picturesque 1790 farm-house that serves as the company's headquarters. The house has almost as colorful a history as the Count. The original saltbox structure served as a girl's school/orphanage until the 1820s when William David Early, of Earlysville fame, purchased the home and added rooms. Early, who lost an arm in the Civil War, spent his remaining days in this house with his family.

While the company preserves the past, it continues to move forward on its own historic path. In July 1998, Nimbus became a Technicolor company. Technicolor's relationship with major motion picture studios as well as its distribution services proved to be a successful match with Nimbus' position as a leader in the optical disc industry, and in November 1999, the company officially changed its name to Technicolor Optical Media Services.

TECHNICOLOR MANUFACTURES CDS AND DVDS FOR SOME OF THE TOP HOLLYWOOD STUDIOS.

In the summer of 2000, Technicolor completed an exclusive agreement with Microsoft to manufacture products for Microsoft's new gaming console, Xbox.

In January 2001, Thomson Multimedia, a Paris-based manufacturer of home electronics such as VCR and DVD players, television sets, and cable set top boxes, acquired Technicolor. Thomson markets its products under such well-known names as RCA, GE, and Proscan. The result is a formidable partnership that blends Thomson's hardware with Technicolor manufactured software.

Technicolor has a solid workforce who enjoy stable employment, generous starting salaries, and a competitive benefits package. The company provides training opportunities and college tuition reimbursement for employees, and works with Piedmont Virginia Community College in offering an apprenticeship program for technicians.

Technicolor's staff includes top-notch engineers, technicians, and industry leaders who are in the forefront of DVD technology. The company's technical employees have been responsible for improving operating efficiencies and reducing cost. In addition, the company developed a new proprietary hologram technology that provides one of the most effective deterrents against the problem of CD piracy.

With a strong commitment to the local community, Technicolor allocates donations to fund local health and human welfare services, economic development efforts, and cultural events. Recently the company purchased dictionaries for placement in every Stanardsville primary school classroom. In addition, Technicolor is a major supporter of the new Greene County Library and Senior Center.

It is estimated that there are nearly three million DVD players in the United States today and the company continues to aggressively research avenues to meet the demand of this burgeoning market. Technicolor's current North American market share for DVD-Video is 26 percent. In 2000, the Ruckersville facility generated revenues of $100 million. It is easy to see why Technicolor, long known to be the greatest name in color, is fast becoming the greatest name in DVDs. ■

BADGER FIRE PROTECTION

One of the Charlottesville region's most successful manufacturing companies is also one of its best-kept secrets. Few people know that just north of Airport Road on Route 29 is one of the world's leading manufacturers of portable fire extinguishers. Badger Fire Protection, a company that dates back to the mid-1890s, has long been an innovator when it comes to portable fire extinguishers. In fact, Badger had the second Underwriter's Laboratory listing for a fire extinguisher in the United States. In 1976 the company moved from New Jersey to its present location in Albemarle County and in 1995 became a subsidiary of Kidde PLC, the largest fire protection company in the world.

Economically, Badger has always been a stable company because it is compliance driven. Virtually every state, county, and major city has a fire code that requires businesses to have fire extinguishers on premise. Badger produces and sells these specialized industrial extinguishers to distributors worldwide.

BADGER'S NEW "EXTRA" LINE OF PORTABLE FIRE EXTIGUISHERS.

Badger's line of fire protection products are manufactured from start-to-finish in its 100,000-square-foot facility. In addition to its line of multi-purpose extinguishers, the company has developed a number of specialty extinguishers that are proprietary to Badger. One is a K-class extinguisher that is designed to put out hazardous cooking oil and fat fires in commercial kitchens. Another Badger innovation is Halotron I. The discharge from this extinguisher evaporates so there is no messy cleanup, making it ideal for computer areas, data storage, telecommunications, and high-tech clean rooms. The Badger Brigade is considered the best, highest performing, portable fire extinguisher on the market today, ideal for outdoor use in high-hazard applications. In 2000, the company introduced the Badger*Extra* Line. Made of premium materials for optimal performance, these revolutionary extinguishers now account for 30 percent of the company's extinguisher sales and catapulted Badger to becoming the industry leader in portable fire extinguisher manufacturing.

Badger attributes its success to producing and selling high-quality products at competitive prices, a superb marketing and new product development team, and its 165 dedicated employees. Together their efforts have netted an unprecedented 25 percent increase in sales since 1998. Badger employees work in a safe environment, with high morale, a generous starting salary, good benefits, education and promotion opportunities, and a pension plan.

A financially strong company, Badger anticipates double-digit growth well into the future, continuing its 100-year tradition of quality, value, and choice of superior quality fire protection products for markets worldwide. ■

BADGER'S MANAGEMENT TEAM IS COMMITTED TO PRODUCING HIGH QUALITY SAFETY PRODUCTS.

COMPUTER SCIENCES CORPORATION

Computer Sciences Corporation (CSC) is one of the world's leading consulting and information technology services firms. The company began in 1959 as a two-person operation working out of a garage. Today, CSC is a Fortune 500 company with headquarters in El Segundo, California, and offices worldwide. Revenues for the 12 months ending March 2001 were $10.5 billion.

DIVERSE TEAMS OF THE BEST AND BRIGHTEST, CSC EMPLOYEES PUSH THE BOUNDARIES OF WHAT PEOPLE AND TECHNOLOGY CAN ACHIEVE.

CSC came to Charlottesville in 1994 to offer subcontracting services to the National Ground Intelligence Center (NGIC). Like its parent company, CSC-Charlottesville grew quickly and by summer 2000 had over 70 employees providing systems integration, consulting, database management, and software solutions to NGIC and other clients.

CSC-Charlottesville attributes its phenomenal growth to its ability to deliver quality work that ultimately turns clients' dreams and goals into reality. Customer satisfaction is CSC's number one priority. As a result, the company has developed a reputation for credibility and competence that has catapulted its impressive growth.

Teamwork is what CSC is all about. The company employs data-entry personnel, documentation specialists, applications developers, database administrators, database architects, and systems engineers, each selected for having the right blend of technical expertise and outstanding people skills. CSC's standards are high, and the company demands a world-class level of performance from its employees. In return, CSC provides a generous benefits package that is in keeping with a Fortune 500 company. Management has an open-door policy and is responsive to employee needs: believing in empowering individuals, encouraging initiative, and providing opportunities for promotion. And because CSC is a global organization, employees have the opportunity to pursue careers in other parts of the world.

Seeking a more prominent presence in the Charlottesville region, CSC has developed a partnership with the Virginia Piedmont Technology Council (VPTC) and Piedmont Virginia Community College (PVCC) to develop talent from within the Charlottesville area. To accomplish that, CSC, along with VPTC and other information technology companies, works closely with PVCC to influence the kind of curriculum that will address the technology of the future and provide companies like CSC with a pool of highly competent "home-grown" employees. CSC's internship program is another way the company works to keep Charlottesville talent in Charlottesville, offering students the opportunity to get invaluable on-site training in the company's Market Street office.

CSC envisions itself as the flagship corporation in the Charlottesville region. As such, it is committed to giving back to the community that has inspired its success by becoming a center of excellence on both the local and global stage. ■

CSC ENCOURAGES A COLLABORATIVE PARTNERSHIP WITH OPEN COMMUNICATION BETWEEN SENIOR MANAGERS AND EMERGING TALENT.

CHARLOTTESVILLE GAS
■ ■ ■ ■ ■

Imagine what it was like to stroll the streets of Charlottesville in 1856. One could see lights flickering from gas street lamps, and a warm glow emanating from decorative gas wall-mounted lamps visible through the windowpanes of private homes. It was in 1856 that Charlottesville and University Gas and Light Company began providing gas to light streets, and to heat and

RESIDENTIAL GAS SERVICE BEING INSTALLED IN NEW ALBEMARLE COUNTY SUBDIVISION. *PHOTO BY DJ MANAFI*

light homes. The site was located on what was appropriately called Gas Plant Road, now 4th Street NW, in an area now known as City Yard. The City of Charlottesville acquired ownership in 1876 and continues to operate Charlottesville Gas today.

During the early 20th century, natural gas supply lines began to be distributed throughout the United States. Tapping into those lines in 1951, Charlottesville Gas began providing area customers with natural gas piped from the Gulf States. According to the Gas Association, there is still plenty of untapped domestic gas, making it a reliable source of energy for years to come.

Charlottesville Gas receives natural gas from the Free Union gate station at Buck Mountain. Gas supply lines silently deliver service to approximately 16,500 residential and commercial customers, including the University of Virginia. The utility has 276 miles of underground gas mains, providing all-weather reliability that is impervious to outages caused by lighting strikes or ice storms. The City's gas service area stretches north along the Route 29 corridor almost to the Albemarle County border, east to Keswick Hall, south to Mill Creek, and west to Farmington. It also serves the North Fork and Fontaine Research Parks and is prepared for future development in these areas.

Recently, Charlottesville Gas completed an ambitious project of replacing pipelines and meters throughout the entire system, including lines that followed the old trolley tracks on Main Street. The utility continually conducts ongoing leak detection surveys to ensure customer safety. As part of its overall operating efficiency, automatic meter reading provides an accurate, convenient, and efficient way of measuring usage.

Knowing that consumers have a choice of energy providers, Charlottesville Gas takes customer service very seriously. Personal assistance is available 24 hours a day, 7 days a week, with well-trained, well-supervised employees rapidly responding to customer needs.

It's no secret, when it comes to selecting an environmentally friendly source of energy, Charlottesville's businesses and homeowners turn to natural gas for unbeatable performance and cost savings. Now the fourth oldest municipal gas operation in the United States, Charlottesville Gas will continue to be as dependable a source of energy today and tomorrow as it was nearly 150 years ago. ■

CHARLOTTESVILLE GAS SUPPLY LINES QUIETLY PROVIDING RELIABLE, EFFICIENT ENERGY THROUGH RURAL ALBEMARLE COUNTY. *PHOTO BY DJ MANAFI, PHOTO OPPOSITE PAGE BY PHILIP BEAURLINE*

12 | CHAPTER **TWELVE**

Marketplace

· · · · · ·

PHOTO BY PHILIP BEAURLINE

DOUBLETREE HOTEL

"Best place to work. Best place to stay." Those eight words express the spirit, commitment, and dedication of the staff of Charlottesville's DoubleTree Hotel. The moment you walk through the lobby doors, you realize this hotel is far from ordinary. For return guests, a stay at the DoubleTree is like coming home. The building exudes a warmth and friendliness that is reflected in the staff's smiles and willingness to lend a hand. Besides, who wouldn't feel at home after receiving the DoubleTree's savory signature greeting—warm, freshly baked, melt-in-your-mouth chocolate chip cookies served upon check-in?

Everything about the DoubleTree makes it the ideal choice for both business and leisure travelers. Its northside location offers something for everyone. For those looking for a quiet respite amid nature's beauty, the hotel is sequestered on a secluded, wooded knoll with peaceful views of the Rivanna River. For those who prefer easy access to Charlottesville's many amenities, the hotel's location on Route 29, just four miles from the Charlottesville/Albemarle Regional Airport, puts restaurants, shopping, and historical sites within an easy drive.

A spacious and handsomely furnished nine-story hotel with 235 guest rooms and executive suites, the DoubleTree has the distinction of being Charlottesville's largest conference facility. With over 16,000 square feet of meeting and banquet space that can accommodate over 1,000 people, the hotel has been able to attract large groups to Charlottesville who might otherwise have gone to another city. Organizations who have chosen to meet at the DoubleTree have reported higher than usual attendance and have attributed that factor to the hotel's excellent service and its accessibility to the area's many historic sites, cultural programs, and spectacular scenery. Locals appreciate the amenities of the DoubleTree as well. The lower-level Promenade Ballroom with its classic woodworking and floor-to-ceiling windows overlooking the tree-lined Rivanna River has made the DoubleTree "the" place in town to have a wedding.

The DoubleTree prides itself on its exemplary customer service. The proof is in the doing at the DoubleTree. Management has put together a mix of talented people who are truly passionate about their work. Each understands that good customer service is about getting back to the basics: greeting guests with a smile, making them feel welcome, giving them a good clean room, and taking care of problems should they arise. The fact that the hotel is seeing an upturn in repeat business is a testament to the staff's mastery of the art of customer service.

The DoubleTree offers its guests two tennis courts; Jacuzzi Suites; a well-equipped exercise facility; volleyball and horseshoes; a business center; in-room movies; an indoor heated pool with whirlpools; a sunny, riverside outdoor pool; a private concierge floor; in-room hair dryers; and in-room ironing boards and irons. The Treetops Restaurant, overlooking the Rivanna River, offers casual dining for breakfast, lunch, and dinner. The Jefferson Lounge is a comfortable place to unwind, enjoy a cocktail, and relax while enjoying the scenic view of the countryside.

The DoubleTree is part of the Hilton Family. As such, hotel guests are able to take advantage of Hilton Honors, considered the best program available for frequent flyer/frequent mile points and the only hotel recognition program that rewards you with points and miles.

During its peak season, the DoubleTree employs close to 150 men and women who blend well with each other, creating a working environment that is comfortable and relaxed. Workers relate to each other in a unique family-oriented atmosphere that combines responsibility with fun. The hotel operates very much as a democracy. The General Manager has an "open door" policy that is rarely seen in the hospitality industry today. On any given day, it's not unusual to see housekeepers and front desk managers in his office exchanging ideas and discussing challenges with him. Monthly luncheons enable employees to share ideas, complaints, suggestions, and concerns. Most importantly, employees are empowered to make decisions on their own, enabling them to respond quicker to customer needs. Career opportunities are abundant, and training is made available to anyone who wishes to advance their career in hotel management.

The management of the DoubleTree is mindful of its place on Monticello's front doorstep and is committed to doing its part to promote community programs. Active in the Tourism Council and in the Chamber of Commerce, the DoubleTree has assumed a leadership role in the development of a new hotel/restaurant association. The hotel has sponsored fund-raisers for Ronald McDonald House and the American Red Cross, and has hosted the March of

Dimes Chef Auction for the past several years. By developing partnerships with business and civic groups as well as nonprofit organizations, the hotel maintains an active role in community affairs.

From the physical beauty of its space to the pride and passion of its staff, the DoubleTree Hotel has created a recipe for success that has indeed made it the "Best place to work; Best place to stay." ◼

KESWICK HALL AT MONTICELLO

■ ■ ■ ■ ■

If one were to replicate the magnificent estates of the past, the comfortable warmth of an English country house, the timeless elegance of Italian Renaissance and French Provincial décor all in one property, it may come close to capturing Orient-Express Hotels' Keswick Hall at Monticello. Consistently named among Conde Nast Traveler magazine's "Best Small Hotels in the World," this Tuscan-style villa situated on 600 pastoral acres bordering the Blue Ridge Mountains, is a unique and intimate hideaway for romantics and explorers.

Keswick Hall's history dates to pre-Civil War when Broad Oak mansion stood on the site. In 1912, the Villa Crawford was built as a private residence and in 1939 became the Clubhouse for the newly formed Keswick Country Club. Purchased in 1990 by Sir Bernard Ashley of the Laura Ashley Design Empire, the property was restored and expanded. In 1999, the resort was acquired by Orient-Express, famous for its worldwide luxury

PHOTO BY PHILIP BEAURLINE

hotels, and legendary trains and cruises. Being associated with Orient-Express provides many exciting benefits and opportunities for Keswick Club members and employees alike, including possible upgrades and amenities at all of its 36 leisure properties worldwide. The portfolio now includes 26 hotels, 6 tourist trains, 2 restaurants, and a river cruise ship, as well as its part ownership of PeruRail, the sole provider of rail services in central and southern Peru.

The Keswick Estate is divided into three areas: Keswick Hall at Monticello, Keswick Club, and Keswick Estates. Keswick Hall's 48 individually furnished guestrooms reflect a particular theme. Facing either formal gardens at the front or the golf course and lush rolling fields at the back, each room is tastefully decorated with antiques, porcelain, and original works of art. Designed to feel more like a home than a hotel, the Hall's public rooms afford guests with additional space to relax, read, play games, or enjoy scones and fresh berries with afternoon tea.

Smaller than most luxury hotels, Keswick Hall's exclusivity, security, comfort, convenience, and attentive yet unobtrusive staff, has made it a favorite among such notables as Margaret Thatcher, Paul Newman, Robert Redford, and Anthony Hopkins. Guests are greeted at the door by name, and check-in is done ensuite. At Keswick Hall, guests experience American hospitality at its best.

With its naturally beautiful surroundings, luxurious guestrooms, exciting leisure facilities, and sophisticated technology, Keswick Hall is the ideal setting for board meetings, social events, corporate retreats, and executive conferences. Intimate weddings and receptions are a specialty at Keswick Hall. The hotel has become famous for its cross-cultural wedding programs designed for travelers who come to Keswick for their wedding and

PHOTO BY PHILIP BEAURLINE

PHOTO BY PHILIP BEAURLINE

honeymoon. Japanese nuptials at Keswick Hall are very special; following the ceremony a tree representing marriage is planted. A plaque with the couple's name and wedding date is placed on the tree. It is believed that as the tree grows, so does the marriage.

Dining at Keswick Hall and Club reflects the estate's eclectic flavor. The Dining Room serves breakfast and dinner daily in a combination classic European/American style with fresh regional produce, and a superb and extensive collection of fine wines from around the world. The Palmer Room, with its sweeping views of the meticulously maintained golf course, offers a more casual dining experience. And during the spring/summer season, light meals are served alfresco at the Pool Pavilion.

The private Keswick Club, open to members and hotel guests only, overlooks an 18-hole golf course designed by Arnold Palmer, who called it "the best greens in Virginia, probably the East Coast." Club facilities also include a driving range, putting green, clay and all-weather tennis courts, an indoor/outdoor swimming pool, a Tuscan-tiled Olympic-sized outdoor pool, extensive health and fitness equipment, as well as massage and body spa treatments.

A new venture for Orient-Express is residential real estate. Keswick Estates is divided into two- to five-acre lots that are earmarked for luxury single-family homes. Families who purchase a home in Keswick Estate are eligible for membership in the Keswick Club.

Although Keswick attracts guests from all over the world, it is also ideal for residents of the region. In addition to wonderful events and dining opportunities, it is perfect for those in need of a relaxing weekend filled with incomparable pampering.

As it embarks on a renaissance of its own, Keswick Hall and Club is committed to maintaining an intimate, luxury hotel of grand style where guests revel in the highest standards of comfort and service synonymous with Orient-Express Hotels.

For more information, please visit www.orient-expresshotels.com. ◼

PHOTO BY PHILIP BEAURLINE

HARRISON AD SERVICE INC.

In 1964, when Bob Harrison decided to go into the advertising specialty business, little did he realize he was starting a family company. With a wife and three young children to support, Bob packed his old Plymouth with promotional samples and headed out on the road, calling on businesses along the way. His one-man road show became a family business when his wife Jane left her teaching job in 1976 to handle the company's administrative work.

Although the Harrisons never pressured their children to join the business, son Rob remembers accompanying his dad on customer calls when he was a youngster. Later, when Rob wanted spending money, Bob suggested he sell ice scrapers. That early indoctrination paid off, and, in 1982, Rob Harrison became the first of his siblings to join the business. His sister Tamra, who was a graphic designer, came on board in 1992.

ROB AND BOB HARRISON. *PHOTO BY RICK BRITTON*

In a world where businesses come and go, Harrison Ad Service attributes its longevity to its commitment to customer service and satisfaction. Many of the businesses that Harrison called upon in 1964 still buy from the company today. That is because the Harrisons continue to provide personal service to their customers, taking the time to understand their businesses so they can suggest the most effective way to get their message across—be it on pens, T-shirts, mouse pads, or incentive programs.

Harrison Ad Service has worked out of its Meade Avenue location since 1990. In addition to offices for staff, the company has sample rooms with hundreds of promotional products on display and offers its clients on-line company stores, fulfillment, and warehousing.

Over the years, the Harrisons have witnessed many changes. Today they work with 165 vendors and a nationwide customer base. While artwork has become more sophisticated, products more innovative, and productivity streamlined, the Harrisons still believe in the same old-fashioned principles upon which they built their success. Personal service and customer satisfaction are still top priority.

As the second generation of Harrisons assumes the company reins, the third generation has already expressed an interest in the business, assuring that Harrison Ad Service Inc. will remain one of Charlottesville's most prized family businesses well into the 21st century. ■

FROM LEFT, ROB HARRISON, JANE HARRISON, BOB HARRISON, TAMRA HARRISON KIRSCHNICK, DANA KIRSCHNICK, AND ELIZABETH WOODSON. *PHOTO BY RICK BRITTON*

CLIFTON—THE COUNTRY INN & ESTATE

■ ■ ■ ■ ■

When guests walk through the doors of the Clifton Inn, they immediately get a sense of what it was like to be a part of 18th century Virginian society. From its impeccably furnished public rooms, gracious accommodations, and award-winning cuisine, this historic 18th century national landmark is the epitome of Southern hospitality.

And that's as it should be, considering this was once the home of one of Virginia's most famous sons— Thomas Mann Randolph (1768-1828), a governor-of Virginia, member of the U.S. Congress, and husband of Thomas Jefferson's daughter, Martha. Built in 1799 to serve as a trading center on the nearby Rivanna River, the house exemplifies federal and colonial revival style architecture. Located within minutes of Monticello, Clifton served as a private residence until 1985 when the current owners restored the property and opened it as a country inn.

Relaxing views of the 70-acre estate's woodlands, gardens, or private lake are visible from each of Clifton's 14 antique-appointed rooms. Luxury amenities abound, including Italian linens, down pillows and comforters, cotton-waffle bathrobes, wood-burning fireplaces, and fresh flowers.

Clifton's recreational facilities—including a clay tennis court, award-winning swimming pool with cascading waterfall, year-round heated whirlpool spa, and croquet pitch—have been carefully designed to blend with the property's natural surroundings.

Renowned for its creative cuisine, every meal at Clifton is a celebration of culinary excellence. A European-style continental breakfast buffet, as well as a hearty daily breakfast entrée, is served each morning on

CLIFTON— THE COUNTRY INN: A "TRUE SOUTHERN LADY"—*THE WASHINGTON POST.*

the sun-filled verandah. Afternoon tea is complemented by delicate pastries and savory finger sandwiches.

Each evening, a pre-dinner cocktail reception with complimentary hors d'oeuvres is held in the drawing room where Clifton's acclaimed chef personally provides a detailed description of each course. The signature *prix fixe* menu is served in a romantic, candlelit style in the historic dining room and is complemented by a perfectly selected bottle of vintage wine from Clifton's mahogany-paneled wine cellar.

The Clifton Inn is a Charlottesville treasure. Its captivating charm has made it one of the most sought-after locations for weddings and special events, and businesses are finding it to be the perfect venue for small corporate meetings and executive retreats. But it's the personalized service at Clifton that really sets it apart. With a 2 to 1 employee-to-guest ratio, the well-seasoned staff provides the kind of attention to detail that is the envy of the industry.

A recipient of the 2001 MobileTravel Guide Four-Star Award and with an AAA Four Diamond rating, the Clifton Inn well deserves its recognition as one of the "premier outstanding establishments in North America." ■

"THE CARRIAGE HOUSE"—A SPACIOUS, LUXURIOUS BI-LEVEL SUITE SURROUNDED BY LUSH FLOWER GARDENS AND PRIVATE JACUZZI.

RED ROOF INN

■ ■ ■ ■ ■

Location. Location. Location. For a hotel, that's the golden ring. Just ask the guests of the Red Roof Inn. Ideally situated on West Main Street in the heart of historic Charlottesville, the hotel is within walking distance of the University of Virginia, the Health Sciences Center, and the Downtown Mall. Open since May 1997 after a yearlong renovation process, the Red Roof Inn has filled a niche by providing an inexpensive lodging alternative that previously did not exist in the downtown Charlottesville area.

Red Roof Inn's philosophy is to provide guests with a clean, comfortable room at the best possible price. Consequently, guests won't find the kind of frills that add to the price of a room. What they will find are 135 beautifully decorated, exceptionally clean and spacious rooms, with complimentary local and 800 phone calls, coffee and tea service in the lobby, laundry and valet service, free parking, and access to Gold's Gym.

The hotel has two on-site restaurants. Chesapeake Bagel Bakery serves a health-conscious breakfast and lunch. The Mellow Mushroom, open for lunch and dinner, specializes in gourmet pizza, calzones, salads, hoagies, and serves both beer and wine. Both restaurants offer catering services.

A WARM FRIENDLY ENVIRONMENT GREETS GUESTS OF THE CHARLOTTESVILLE RED ROOF INN, WHERE THEY CAN ALSO ENJOY COMPLIMENTARY COFFEE AND TEA SERVICE IN THE LOBBY.

Business travelers especially appreciate the hotel's executive rooms. While all rooms are equipped with voice mail and data ports, Business King rooms have the added convenience of speakerphones and a large work desk. For those looking for meeting space, the Red Roof Inn features two personable conference rooms: The Commonwealth Boardroom, which seats 10 to 12 people, and the Old Dominion Conference Room that can accommodate up to 35.

The Red Roof Inn employs 35 full-time people who work together to create an atmosphere that is informal, friendly, and family-oriented. Everyone at Red Roof Inns goes out of their way to make sure a guest's stay is as pleasant as possible, even under the most trying circumstances. This is especially true for guests with a family member in the hospital. As an extra convenience for these guests, the hospital provides a shuttle between the hospital and the hotel. The hotel has a history of supporting health-related charities and has participated in the Children's Miracle Network, Multiple Sclerosis Society fundraisers, and the AIDS walk.

The Charlottesville Red Roof Inn is one of 350 inns nationwide owned by Accor Economy Lodging, the largest owner and operator of economy lodging properties in the U.S. With 98 percent of guests indicating they would return, Red Roof Inns give travelers one more reason to "Always Stop at Red." ■

CONVENIENTLY LOCATED ON WEST MAIN STREET, THE 135-ROOM CHARLOTTESVILLE RED ROOF INN FEATURES INTERIOR CORRIDORS, TWO ON-SITE RESTAURANTS AND TWO CONFERENCE ROOMS.

RAPID PHOTOS

In 1982, one-hour labs were a new concept in the field of photo processing. Recognizing the enormous potential of this business, Maryland-native John Thompson moved to Charlottesville and opened Rapid Photos, Central Virginia's first one-hour photo processing lab.

Rapid Photos offers one-hour photo processing and digital printing, producing prints ranging in size from wallets to 44-inch-wide enlargements. With its remarkable digital capability, Rapid Photos provides a wide range of specialty work, including adding and deleting images on existing photos, and restoring old photographs that have been discolored, folded, or stained. Other specialties include custom photo greeting cards, business cards, and Christmas cards.

From the beginning, Rapid Photos was built on two principles: quality products and unparalleled customer service. Over the last 20 years, while one-hour labs found their way into convenient stores, drug stores, and supermarkets, Rapid Photos retained its competitive edge by earning a reputation for quality and service that made it the preferred choice of amateur and professional photographers alike.

Most Rapid Photos employees have been with the business for years and have developed friendly relationships with regular customers. Because everyone at Rapid Photos loves photography, they go the extra mile to make sure the pictures they process turn out right. With state-of-the-art equipment and the skilled personnel who know how to use it, Rapid Photos excels at quality control.

Each print is examined and when it's not up to par, customers are told why and offered suggestions on how to get better results next time. It's that kind of personal service that has enabled Rapid Photos to succeed.

Rapid Photos prides itself on being ahead of the technological curve in photo processing. Taking advantage of the endless possibilities of digital photography, Rapid Photos' future plans include providing stations for customers to print their own digital images. Wide-format photography will enable Rapid Photos to expand further into corporate advertising. And fun projects such as the development of family collages and personalized memorabilia will be among Rapid Photos' more creative pursuits.

Rapid Photos believes that quality work and service is what Charlottesville is all about and, with that in mind, is very discriminating in its choice of photo accessories. Handsome albums and classically designed frames line the shelves, each selected for its quality, durability, and timelessness.

Located in a place that is synonymous with quality—the north wing of the Barracks Road Shopping Center—Rapid Photos remains committed to producing quality images that enrich lives, rekindle heartwarming memories, and most of all, make people smile. ■

13 CHAPTER THIRTEEN

BUSINESS & FINANCE

· · · · ·

PHOTO BY PHILIP BEAURLINE

STATE FARM INSURANCE

■ ■ ■ ■ ■

THE UNITED WAY DAY OF CARING ATTRACTS DOZENS OF WILLING VOLUNTEERS FROM STATE FARM.

Like a good neighbor, State Farm is there. Millions of people recognize those words as the slogan for the State Farm Insurance Companies, but for the 2,500 plus employees who are based out of the eastern regional office on Pantops Mountain, those words are a way of life.

State Farm has been a good neighbor to Virginians since 1930 when the company first started selling auto policies in the state. Within five years it had become the largest insurer in Virginia, a position it maintains to this day. The company's first regional office opened on Emmet Street in June 1952 and moved into its current headquarters in December 1979. This office underwrites and services auto, fire, life, and health policies for customers in Virginia and North Carolina and is the largest private employer in the Charlottesville region.

With an impressively low turnover rate, State Farm has earned the enviable reputation as one of the best places to work in Charlottesville. One need only look at the wall of photos honoring employees with 35 plus years of service to realize that the company is doing something right to foster such loyalty. Some State Farm employees are third generation and many have relatives who work there. In addition to those who live in Charlottesville and Albemarle County, State Farm employees reside in six surrounding counties. To help ease the long drive into town and save money, pollution, and parking spaces, the company purchased two dozen vans and organized employee carpools. It is just one way the company looks out for its people.

State Farm is a company whose culture is designed to nurture and empower its employees. The company's structure resembles an upside down pyramid with customers at the top and the chairman of the board at the bottom. Despite having different jobs and responsibilities, everyone is on a first name basis. Working in that kind of environment, it is no wonder that State Farm employees are considered some of the nicest people in town. This is especially comforting to policyholders whose only interaction with the company may be during a time of duress. Caring, compassionate people who do their job well is the cornerstone upon which the company has grown.

Yet State Farm does much more than care for its own. An active participant in community affairs, the company has initiated numerous programs that have greatly benefited the area. A founding member of The Charlottesville Albemarle School/Business Alliance,

STATE FARM'S EASTERN REGIONAL OFFICE ON PANTOPS MOUNTAIN.

INDIVIDUAL EMPLOYEES HAVE THE SUPPORT OF THEIR COMPANY WHEN THEY VOLUNTEER IN LOCAL SCHOOLS.

State Farm's generosity grows out of the company's unprecedented success since its founding in Bloomington, Illinois, in 1922. Back then, company founder George J. Mecherle came up with the novel idea that farmers driving on rural roads should not have to pay the same auto insurance rates as drivers in Chicago. For the first seven years, the company only sold auto policies, adding life insurance in 1929, fire insurance in 1935, and health insurance in 1965. Throughout the years, the company's ever-evolving product and service lines have kept the company moving forward. Most recently, State Farm made its greatest leap when it broke the insurance-only mold by establishing The State Farm Bank and selling mutual funds to its customers.

No doubt Mr. Mecherle would be pleased to see how his company has grown from helping farmers on rural Illinois roads to offering full financial services to the 30 million households it now protects nationwide. With a claims center that is second to none, a dedicated, quality workforce that is valued by management, and a working environment designed to retain people for a lifetime, State Farm is indeed a good neighbor to the Charlottesville region. ◼

a collaboration between the schools, the Chamber of Commerce, University of Virginia, Piedmont Virginia Community College, and area businesses, State Farm has worked tirelessly in support of education. For example, the company supplied a $25,000 grant to equip a school bus with lap top computers and other educational tools. The bus travels to low-income neighborhoods each day to enable area children to work on computers and get help with their homework. Through its Educational Support Policy, the company gives its employees an annual paid day off to volunteer in the schools. Its Book Buddies Program provides employee volunteers to tutor children in reading. The company also is highly active in Junior Achievement and United Way's Day of Caring. And to further promote volunteerism, for those employees who make a commitment of 40 hours per year to a nonprofit organization, the company donates $500 to that organization in the employee's name.

While State Farm encourages volunteerism among its employees, it also supports the community through sizable capital donations. The company has helped fund improvements at Martha Jefferson and the University of Virginia Hospitals; the Darden School; the downtown Amphitheater; and the bridge at Monticello, to name just a few.

PROVIDING FRIENDLY, GOOD NEIGHBOR SERVICE IS THE COMPANY'S CORNERSTONE.

CHARLOTTESVILLE REGIONAL CHAMBER OF COMMERCE

The Charlottesville Regional Chamber of Commerce is a private business member alliance dedicated to representing private enterprise, promoting business, and enhancing the quality of life in the greater Charlottesville community. The chamber represents 1,400 member businesses and organizations, which together employ more than 45,000 people in the area. Even a modest estimate of just the direct economic impact of that level of employment converts to more than $1.3 billion in annual payroll alone. The chamber is the voice of business.

CHAMBER NETWORKING EVENTS ARE HELD ON A MONTHLY BASIS. THEY PROVIDE A CASUAL AND COMFORTABLE VENUE FOR THE SHARING OF INFORMATION, BUSINESS TRENDS, AND CONTACTS.

A Little History

As early as 1911, business owners in Charlottesville recognized the advantage of getting together to discuss common needs and concerns. Meeting at Timberlake's Drug Store, these visionaries decided to form a chamber of commerce to represent Charlottesville businesses, which at the time existed mainly in the downtown area and on West Main Street. In 1913, the Charlottesville Chamber of Commerce became one of the earliest chambers to be officially incorporated in the Commonwealth of Virginia.

By the 1960s there were enough operating businesses in Albemarle County to warrant the chamber changing its name to the Charlottesville-Albemarle Chamber of Commerce. Over the next 30 years, the focus shifted to businesses, employees, and customers coming in from Madison, Greene, Orange, Louisa, Fluvanna, and Nelson counties. In 1998 in an effort to encompass its entire trading area and reflect its broader scope, the chamber changed its name once more to the Charlottesville Regional Chamber of Commerce.

The Chamber Today and Tomorrow

The communities that make up the Charlottesville region are blessed with enthusiastic, dedicated men and women who recognize how vital it is to future generations to maintain the economic vitality and quality of life they have come to enjoy. Representatives from diverse member businesses have traditionally worked well together. This has enabled the chamber to create effective private-public partnerships, among the strongest being the bond between the business community and the region's educational system.

Responding to businesses' need for a flexible, technology-savvy, 21st century workforce, the chamber joined with Albemarle and Fluvanna County schools, Charlottesville public schools, Piedmont Virginia Community College (PVCC) and the University of Virginia (U.Va.) to form the Charlottesville Area School Business Alliance (CASBA). The chamber works with the university to help market its modern research parks with both local entrepreneurs and outside technology businesses that wish to grow in the Charlottesville region. The chamber works in partnership with the Virginia Piedmont Technology Council toward fostering an environment where entrepreneurs, especially those

THE CHAMBER'S BOARD OF DIRECTORS MAKES POLICY FOR THE CHAMBER OF COMMERCE IN RESPONSE TO THE MEMBERSHIP. THE EXECUTIVE COMMITTEE AND THE BOARD MEET REGULARLY.

specializing in information technologies, can find the resources they need to thrive in this region. Other partnerships— the Small Business Development Center, the Service Corps of Retired Executives (SCORE), the Thomas Jefferson Partnership for Economic Development— and the Business Education Roundtable, are similarly focused.

Recognizing the impact that legislation has on business and the community, the chamber is also an active advocate for business on a range of local, state, and federal public policy matters.

Tourism is another arena in which the chamber is active. Along with the City of Charlottesville and Albemarle County, the chamber helps direct the Charlottesville-Albemarle Convention & Visitors Bureau. Through its travel and tourism promotional efforts, the bureau blends the interests of regional businesses and government to bring more visitors, meetings, and events to the Charlottesville region.

With neighboring counties impacted by the influx of newcomers into the area, the Charlottesville Regional Chamber of Commerce reaches out to other area chambers in nearby counties to share resources and assist with developing strategies.

PETER RICE, PRESIDENT AND FOUNDER OF PLOW & HEARTH, SPEAKS WITH CHAMBER PRESIDENT TIMOTHY HULBERT AT THE GRAND RE-OPENING OF PLOW & HEARTH'S LOCAL RETAIL STORE. THE CHAMBER IS ACTIVE IN THE PROMOTION OF BOTH ITS LARGE AND SMALL BUSINESS MEMBERS.

KEITH CHEATHAM, PUBLIC POLICY MANAGER OF THE VIRGINIA CHAMBER OF COMMERCE, SPEAKS AT A CHARLOTTESVILLE REGIONAL CHAMBER OF COMMERCE NEWS CONFERENCE. THE CHAMBER IS AN ACTIVE "VOICE OF BUSINESS" IN A RANGE OF PUBLIC POLICY ISSUES RELATING TO PRIVATE ENTERPRISE AND THE ECONOMY.

Chamber member businesses and organizations have a generous menu of member services to choose from, each designed to aid in their business pursuits. The chamber provides customer referrals to members, promotional opportunities, business workshops, and cooperative buying discounts on long-distance service. Members also are able to participate in leadership, educational, and community development programs, and be a part of ongoing efforts to expand local businesses, tourism, and economic development. Of course, networking opportunities, such as "Business After Hours" and other social events, enable members to make those all-important business and customer contacts.

For 90 years, the Charlottesville Regional Chamber of Commerce has been the region's premier business and civic alliance. The chamber is a leading community force. With an insightful board of directors and the selfless efforts of countless members, that same visionary leadership continues today protecting and developing the economic vitality and quality of life of the greater Charlottesville communities and will do so well into the 21st century. ∎

UNIVERSITY OF VIRGINIA COMMUNITY CREDIT UNION

It may sound like a worn-out cliché, but it's true. The University of Virginia Community Credit Union is the epitome of what a credit union is all about—people helping people. Here customers are called "members," and each member owns a share of the company. The Board of Directors, elected by the membership, is a group of dedicated, committed volunteers. And even though there are over 37,000 members, everyone is treated as if they were the organization's most valuable asset.

And in truth, they are. The UVA Community Credit Union operates from the core belief that everyone has the right to affordable alternative banking. Originally established in 1954 to offer financial services for university hospital employees, the credit union now holds a community charter and its services are available to everyone living in Charlottesville or Albermarle, Greene or Fluvanna counties. Branches are located on Berkmar Drive, Arlington Boulevard, High Street, the UVA Hospital parking garage, and the newest on Pantops Mountain.

Although voted the "best bank" in Charlottesville by readers of *Charlottesville Weekly* in its "Best of Charlottesville" survey, the UVA Community Credit Union is not a bank at all. It is a member-owned, not-for-profit organization that has grown to become the number one consumer lending institution in the area. Popular because of its low-cost services, such as a no-fee interest-bearing checking account, the Credit Union is known foremost for its unique method of

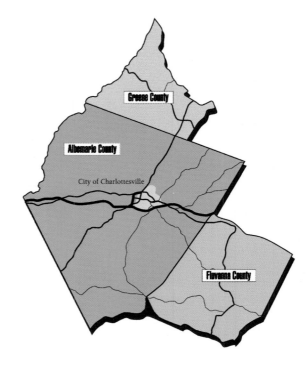

UVA COMMUNITY CREDIT UNION MEMBERSHIP IS OPEN TO ALL WHO LIVE, WORK, OR ATTEND SCHOOL IN THE CITY OF CHARLOTTESVILLE OR THE COUNTIES OF ALBEMARLE, FLUVANNA, AND GREENE.

lending money to people in need. Whether it's a home mortgage or auto loan, or a small emergency loan to get the electricity turned on or buy a refrigerator, the Credit Union responds quickly to its members' needs. Most lending is done over the phone, and in some cases money is deposited in a member's account within hours.

The relationship with members has always been special; so special, in fact, that members have been more than willing to share their positive experiences in a member testimonial campaign. Being in sync with member needs is a matter of pride for the Credit Union. Periodic member surveys are done to encourage feedback. From these come new products and services, from free financial educational seminars to phone and on-line account accessing programs.

It's that kind of personal commitment—people helping people—that has made the UVA Community Credit Union such a valued and stable force in the community for nearly 50 years. ■

BREAKING GROUND FOR THE CREDIT UNION'S NEWEST BRANCH AT PANTOPS ARE JEFFREY C. MOSCICKI, CHAIRMAN, ALISON DETUNCQ, PRESIDENT AND CEO (FRONT LEFT), AS WELL AS DIRECTORS, BOARD COMMITTEE CHAIRMEN, AND THE ALBEMARLE COUNTY EXECUTIVE.

BB&T

■ ■ ■ ■ ■

When Thomas Jefferson Hadley co-founded the organizational ancestor of Branch Banking & Trust back in 1872, he surely never imagined that BB&T would one day serve his famous namesake's hometown.

LEFT TO RIGHT: J. SPENCER BIRDSONG, V.P.—COMMERCIAL BANKING; IVY GRAY, FINANCIAL CENTER LEADER; BRYAN E. THOMAS, CITY EXECUTIVE—SR. V.P.; PATRICIA FLANAGAN, A.V.P.—FINANCIAL CENTER LEADER; COBY FRYE, A.V.P.—BUSINESS BANKING MANAGER.

Founded in the eastern North Carolina farm town of Wilson, BB&T survived the panics, wars, and the Great Depression that followed. Today, it is a $70 billion organization offering banking, insurance, leasing, mortgage lending, and brokerage services. With more than 1,000 branches in eight states and Washington, D.C., BB&T is the country's 17th largest financial institution, a ranking it achieved through prudent growth, unmatched client service, loyal decision-making, and a clearly defined set of values.

The unique BB&T Philosophy is widely recognized and respected in the industry. In its continuing quest to be "The Best of the Best," BB&T pursues its relationships with clients, employees, shareholders, and the community with a vision that incorporates the ancient wisdom of philosophers such as Aristotle. That unorthodox, but highly successful approach to business is outlined in the company's impressive corporate philosophy booklet. It spells out topics such as "independent thinking," "honesty," "integrity," "justice," "pride," and "teamwork."

The company's stated desire "to make the world a better place to live" was evident from the moment it entered the Charlottesville/Albemarle market in November 2000. Upon its merger with One Valley and its purchase of divested branches from Central Fidelity and Jefferson National Bank, BB&T not only offered positions to employees from those banks, it created new jobs as well. With no layoffs, the merger was seamless for customers and employees alike.

BB&T may be a large financial institution, but it acts very much like a small, community-based bank in its dealings with local organizations and small businesses. A generous provider of corporate donations and sponsorships of local organizations, BB&T is also a reliable source of small business loans. The U.S. Small Business Administration named it the number one "small business friendly" bank in the United States in two of the last three years.

Business Week magazine in 1999 named BB&T as the highest performing commercial bank holding company in the S&P 500 and in the top 10 percent of all S&P 500 companies. And BB&T is recognized on Wall Street as one of the country's safest and soundest financial institutions.

Thanks to BB&T's visionary philosophy and financial strength, it promises to make a viable difference in the Charlottesville region's ever-growing financial landscape. ■

CHARLOTTESVILLE/ALBEMARLE AIRPORT AUTHORITY

∎ ∎ ∎ ∎ ∎

When travelers fly into a city, it is the airport that provides the first impression of what that area has to offer. The Charlottesville-Albemarle Airport is no exception, reflecting the warm and welcoming spirit that is indicative of the Charlottesville-Albemarle region.

In operation since 1955, the Charlottesville-Albemarle Airport is known for passenger convenience, and innovative, cutting-edge services. Situated eight miles north of Charlottesville and one mile west of U.S. Route 29 on State 649, the airport is just minutes from the University of Virginia and surrounding counties. Long and short-term parking lots are within a short walking distance of the terminal so passengers can check-in and get to their gate quickly. With a mountain vista as a backdrop, the airport's dramatic setting outside is equaled by its impressive display of Jeffersonian architecture inside the terminal's Rotunda area. If first impressions were given scores, the Charlottesville-Albemarle Airport would capture a perfect 10 as one of the most efficient, passenger-friendly, and beautiful airports in the country.

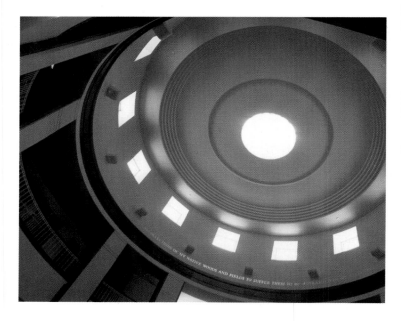

Approximately 375,000 passengers travel through the Charlottesville-Albemarle Airport each year. The airport is served by three airlines—US Airways Express, Comair: Delta Connection, and United Express—offering destinations to more than 500 cities nationwide with nonstop service to and from major hubs in Charlotte, Cincinnati, New York, Philadelphia, Pittsburgh, and Washington, D.C.

Ground transportation is provided by three car rental companies, taxi service, and shuttle van service. Inside the terminal is a food/beverage/gift concession; a business center with work stations; a public fax machine; and a private conference room.

In addition to commercial services, the airport has a state-of-the-art general aviation facility for private aircraft operations and is the home base for Pegasus, the University of Virginia's air ambulance service. Two flight schools offering basic or commercial service pilot's licenses are also based at the airport, as is an aircraft rental company, and three charter services.

The airport employs over 200 people, including a professional rescue and fire fighting team and law enforcement officers whose training and certification exceed FAA standards. That factor, coupled with modern equipment and a technologically advanced radar system, has earned the airport an exceptional safety record.

To accommodate the anticipated future growth of the region, the Airport Authority has adopted a long-term master plan for service and facility improvements through 2014. Yet one thing will remain the same. The Charlottesville-Albemarle Airport will always be "close, convenient, and connected" to everyone who visits or lives in the Charlottesville region. ∎

PHOTO BY PHILIP BEAURLINE

14 | CHAPTER FOURTEEN

PROFESSIONS

·····

PHOTO © JOHN BORGE

McKee Carson

For nearly a quarter of a century, McKee Carson has provided professional services of the highest caliber to private, public, and institutional clients throughout the region. An interdisciplinary firm of land planners, landscape architects, civil engineers, and land development consultants, McKee Carson is based in downtown Charlottesville.

commercial, industrial, institutional, municipal, recreational, and multi-use development endeavors.

Noteworthy local projects include the University of Virginia's Fontaine Research Park, including the widening of Fontaine Avenue, the National Ground Intelligence Center, the Wachovia Bank Operations Center, the Charlottesville Ice Park, and numerous large-scale residential communities. For the University of Virginia, McKee Carson provided all civil engineering and landscape architectural services in the design and construction of the Snyder Tennis Facility. This striking recreational facility is located prominently on the grounds. The Fontaine Research Park employed a depth of services including master planning, rezoning, infrastructure engineering, architectural guidelines, and landscape architecture for this extensive development.

An integrated, coordinated team approach, where varied disciplines freely interact and the client participates actively in the process, is the cornerstone of the firm's design philosophy. McKee Carson is able to produce effective project results by establishing with the client clear program objectives, maintaining high standards of design, maximizing opportunities, and responding creatively to environmental, economic, and regulatory constraints. Through an interplay of professional disciplines, McKee Carson is able to offer to its clients a comprehensive approach to master planning and site development, which integrally addresses the technical, economic, and aesthetic aspects of the project at hand. ■

The company has grown over the years, increasing its staff and adding technologies. Work is performed on state-of-the-art computer systems running a broad range of engineering and design software. Coupled with this technological base is the belief that all of the firm's design and planning endeavors should encourage responsible land stewardship while fostering environments of enduring quality and beauty. The success of this focus is clearly demonstrated in the overwhelming percentage of return clients. McKee Carson understands the tried and true relationship between good planning and design and the creation of economic value.

Its staff of highly trained and experienced professionals enables McKee Carson to respond to projects of any scale and nature, particularly those with unique programmatic objectives and a high level of design and engineering complexity. The firm offers a broad spectrum of design services and professional consultation beginning with initial project feasibility and concept inception through construction oversight and project closeout. Project types include a diversity of residential,

FIELD SPORT CONCEPTS, LTD.

■ ■ ■ ■ ■

For the landowner wishing to retain a "country lifestyle" with its inherent benefits, field sport activities may offer the best of all worlds.

Field sport includes such pursuits as equine sports, fishing and hunting, range shooting, and their amenities. Related activities include certain ball sports, special outdoor events, competitions, wildlife observation, educational seminars, and fairs. The focus of Field Sport Concepts, Ltd., is to assist landowners in preserving and enhancing important rural open lands through the creative implementation of environmentally and economically sound alternatives to traditional land development practices. This approach to the stewardship of rural lands is accomplished through sustainable land-use programs, which emphasize field sport activities and land-use options having minimal impact on rural countryside. In keeping with this objective, the modification of open spaces for sporting uses must involve careful and innovative planning to preserve the land's aesthetic and ecological value.

Field Sport Concepts, Ltd., is an alliance of respected consultants familiar not only with the design and development of diversified field sport facilities and amenities, but also an organization with broad expertise in the fields of resource-based land planning, engineering, architecture, environmental sciences, law, real estate, and other complementary disciplines such as forestry, fisheries, and wildlife management. The organization is backed by an in-house staff of civil and water resource engineers, landscape architects, land planners, and environmental specialists who provide the necessary overall planning, technical, and logistical support.

Services are provided to field sport enthusiasts, farmers, land conservation and preservation organizations, land trusts, resort and preserve owners and operators, other owners of large land holdings such as timber and mineral resource enterprises and utility companies, and land developers with a vision of a unique, amenity-rich community.

Field Sport Concepts, Ltd., provides comprehensive planning and design consultation services pertaining to the following facilities and activities: sporting estates, preserves and clubs, equestrian facilities, shooting sport ranges and courses, hunting environments, fishing venues, and other multi-use, multi-seasonal facilities and events such as recreational sports and ballfields, battle reenactments, dog trials/shows, Scottish games, environmental, education venues, fairs, and other activities associated with rural areas.

Projects undertaken by Field Sport Concepts strive to preserve the natural beauty and resources inherent to the land, encourage the perpetual use of the property for agricultural enterprise, create improved wildlife habitat, increase land values, develop opportunities for income generation, and promote rural recreational pursuits and their attendant lifestyles.

Committed to preserving rural land and the traditions and lifestyles associated with it, Field Sport Concepts, Ltd., offers a fresh approach to rural land preservation. An appreciation and respect for the natural environment and ensuring the future of the sporting life is what Field Sport Concepts is all about. ■

NORTHWESTERN MUTUAL FINANCIAL NETWORK

Northwestern Mutual Financial Network looks at its clients' visions for the future first. An individual's vision says a lot about who they are. And like each client, each vision is unique. So is Northwestern Mutual's approach to helping its clients shape and attain their dreams.

The company's foremost goal is to help these visions become reality. Simply put, its mission is to secure the future of its clients and their families, to make their life better, and to protect what's important to them. Bring Northwestern Mutual a vision and its financial representatives will help make it happen.

Northwestern Mutual has been a part of the Charlottesville community for over 30 years. Like its clients, its representatives live here. They share and understand the values and ideals of this community. As a successful business, it also knows the local environment in which companies operate, and what it takes to succeed. This gives its financial representatives special insight and allows them to help clients plan for their future with these things in mind. The company's focus is always on its clients.

Enduring Relationships

Today, the Northwestern Mutual Financial Network provides sound, effective personal planning and advice to its clients throughout the area. As part of the Northwestern Mutual Financial Network, the Charlottesville group is dedicated to providing expert guidance and innovative solutions to help people identify and meet financial goals at different stages in their lives.

Expert Guidance

Northwestern Mutual's representatives work closely with the network's group of trusted financial specialists in areas like retirement planning, estate planning, investment planning, employee benefits, and small business planning to ensure that each client's needs are looked at from every perspective. This personalized approach leads to customized recommendations that will help a client make decisions that are right for them and those who depend on them.

Innovative Solutions

Representatives offer exclusive access to insurance products and an array of investment choices from Northwestern Mutual, a company that has always received the highest possible financial ratings. In addition, Northwestern Mutual's sales force has been named the "Best Sales Force" in America by *Sales & Marketing Management* magazine, as well as the number one sales force in the life insurance industry each year it has been included in the magazine's survey. This recognition is based on sales performance during the previous three years, reputation for customer satisfaction, and interviews with industry analysts and executives.

Because planning one's financial future can be complicated, and each person's set of circumstances is unique, it's important that everyone have the help of highly trained and experienced professionals. Northwestern Mutual's financial representatives and the specialists they work with have a proven record of expertise and success, and are knowledgeable partners in helping clients plan for a future in which their goals are achieved and their dreams become reality. ■

CHARLOTTESVILLE FINANCIAL REPRESENTATIVES.

THE LEXISNEXIS GROUP

■ ■ ■ ■ ■

While the name LexisNexis is a well-recognized name nationally and is becoming more recognized in the Charlottesville community, its predecessor locally, The Michie Company, is a name most long-time Charlottesville residents know well. Founded in the late 1800s, The Michie Company was acquired in 1994 by Reed Elsevier, a leading world publisher and information provider.

An innovative force in the information industry, LexisNexis pioneered the field of online research in 1973 by introducing the LEXIS® service—the first commercial, full-text legal information service designed to help legal professionals conduct research more efficiently. Today the company is a leader in the legal publishing industry, providing pertinent legal information for legal professionals in law firms, law schools, and the judiciary via the World Wide Web, dial-up online, CD-ROM, and hardcopy print. Locally, the company prints hardcopy books at its Carlton manufacturing site, produces CD-ROM products, and supports the success of Primary Law Publishing.

LexisNexis owns some of the most recognized and authoritative titles in the world and provides unparalleled access to full-text online newspapers, magazines, wire services, and legal material. The company boasts one billion searchable documents—nearly three times the size of the Web. Through the lexis.com research system, customers such as lawyers, journalists, politicians, financial professionals, advertising specialists, marketing experts, and researchers can find, analyze, and validate critical information at a moment's notice.

LEXISNEXIS MAIN BUILDING ON EAST WATER STREET IN CHARLOTTESVILLE.

LexisNexis maintains its leadership in the industry through state-of-the-art products that surpass its competition. One such product is lexisONE.com. Tailored to small law offices, this dynamic new portal delivers free information to legal professionals while providing a link to all other LexisNexis resources.

The Charlottesvile site is the LexisNexis "Center of Excellence for Primary Law Publishing" and employs over 550 people in two area offices. As one of the area's major employers, LexisNexis sees Charlottesville's appeal as an asset in attracting talent to the area. Staffed by some of brightest minds in the industry, the company provides a work environment that is characterized by respect for each individual, where cultural and ethnic diversity are blended by teamwork into a high-performing work force, and creativity and individual initiative are valued and rewarded.

The LexisNexis name is affiliated with many of the key cultural, educational, and humanitarian organizations in the Charlottesville region. The company has a broad community relations program through which corporate contributions, employee volunteerism and campaign efforts, and matching gifts are generated.

With more than two million subscribers in more than 60 countries and high volume in sales worldwide, LexisNexis' pioneering work in online research nearly 30 years ago has paid off in a big way. ■

LEXISNEXIS' MANUFACTURING AND TECHNOLOGY FACILITY LOCATED ON CARLTON AVENUE IN CHARLOTTESVILLE.

ENTERPRISE INDEX
▪ ▪ ▪ ▪ ▪

Badger Fire Protection
4251 Seminole Trail
Charlottesville, Virginia 22911
Phone: (434) 973-4361
Fax: (434) 973-1589
E-mail: vic.modic@badgerfire.com
www.badgerfire.com
Page 118

BB&T
300 Preston Avenue
Charlottesville, Virginia 22902
Phone: (434) 979-2251
Fax: (434) 977-4142
www.bbandt.com
Page 139

Biotage, Inc. A Dyax Corp. Company
P.O. Box 8006
Charlottesville, Virginia 22906
Phone: (434) 979-2319
Fax: (434) 979-4743
www.biotage.com
Pages 112-113

**Charlottesville/Albemarle
Airport Authority**
100 Bowen Loop, Suite 200
Charlottesville, Virginia 22911
Phone: (434) 973-8341
Fax: (434) 974-7476
E-mail: info@gocho.com
www.gocho.com
Page 140

Charlottesville Gas
305 4th Street Northwest
Charlottesville, Virginia 22903
Phone: (434) 970-3800
Fax: (434) 970-3817
www.charlottesville.org
Page 120

**Charlottesville Glass and
Mirror Corporation**
1428 East High Street
Charlottesville, Virginia 22902
Phone: (434) 293-9188
Fax: (434) 977-4362
E-mail: info@charlottesvilleglassandmirror.com
www.charlottesvilleglassandmirror.com
Page 94

**Charlottesville Regional
Chamber of Commerce**
209 5th Street Northeast
Charlottesville, Virginia 22902
Phone: (434) 295-3141
Fax: (434) 295-3144
E-mail: chamber@cvillechamber.com
www.cvillechamber.com
Pages 136-137

Church of the Incarnation
1465 Incarnation Drive
Charlottesville, Virginia 22901
Phone: (434) 973-4381
Fax: (434) 973-1757
E-mail: incarnation@cstone.net
www.incarnationparish.org
Page 106

Clifton - The Country Inn & Estate
1296 Clifton Inn Drive
Charlottesville, Virginia 22911
Phone: (434) 971-1800
Fax: (434) 971-7098
E-mail: reservations@cliftoninn.com
www.cliftoninn.com
Page 129

Computer Sciences Corporation
401 East Market Street
Executive Suites
Charlottesville, Virginia 22902
Phone: (804) 244-6505
Fax: (804) 970-2021
E-mail: cdavis47@csc.com
        jvavoso@csc.com
www.cstone.net/~csc
Page 119

DoubleTree Hotel
990 Hilton Heights Road
Charlottesville, Virginia 22901
Phone: (434) 973-2121
Fax: (434) 978-7735
www.doubletree.com
Pages 124-125

Federal Executive Institute
1301 Emmet Street
Charlottesville, Virginia 22903
Phone: (434) 980-6200
Fax: (434) 979-1030
E-mail: fei@opm.gov
www.leadership.opm.gov/
Page 104

Field Sport Concepts, LTD.
301 East High Street
Charlottesville, Virginia 22902
Phone: (434) 979-3846
Fax: (434) 977-1194
E-mail: info@fieldsport.com
www.fieldsport.com
Page 145

Gaffney Homes
1758-A Worth Park
Charlottesville, Virginia 22911
Phone: (434) 978-1884
Fax: (434) 978-3604
E-mail: mgaffney@gaffneyhomes.com
www.gaffneyhomes.com
Pages 90-91

Harrison Ad Service Inc.
525 Meade Avenue
Charlottesville, Virginia 22902
Phone: (434) 293-5698
Fax: (434) 293-3917
E-mail: service@harrisonad.com
www.harrisonad.com
Page 128

Keswick Hall at Monticello
701 Club Drive
Keswick, Virginia 22947
Phone: (434) 979-3440
Fax: (434) 977-4171
E-mail:keswick@keswick.com
www.keswick.com
Pages 126-127

The LexisNexis Group
P.O. Box 7587
Charlottesville, Virginia 22906-7587
701 East Water Street
Charlottesville, Virginia 22902
Phone: (434) 972-7600
www.lexisnexis.com
Page 147

McKee Carson
301 East High Street
Charlottesville, Virginia 22902
Phone: (434) 979-7522
Fax: (434) 977-1194
E-mail: mc@mckeecarson.com
www.mckeecarson.com
Page 144

MicroAire Surgical Instruments
1641 Edlich Drive
Charlottesville, Virginia 22911
Phone: (434) 975-8000
Fax: (434) 975-4144
E-mail: microaire@microaire.com
www.microaire.com
Pages 114-115

Montague Miller & Co. Realtors
500 Westfield Road
Charlottesville, Virginia 22901
Phone: (434) 973-5393
Fax: (434) 951-7101
E-mail: relo@montaguemiller.com
www.montaguemiller.com
Page 93

Northwestern Mutual Financial Network
675 Peter Jefferson Parkway, Suite 150
Charlottesville, Virginia 22911
Phone: (434) 295-2700
Fax: (434) 817-1065
E-mail: blueridgegroup@northwesternmutual.com
www.nmfn.com/blueridgegroup
Page 146

R.D. Wade Builder, Inc.
P.O. Box 7506
Charlottesville, Virginia 22906
Phone: (434) 973-7841
Fax: (434) 973-9672
Page 92

Rapid Photos
2160 Barracks Road
Charlottesville, Virginia 22903
Phone: (434) 979-0777
Fax: (434) 977-6066
www.rapidphotos.net
Page 131

Red Roof Inn
1309 West Main Street
Charlottesville, Virginia 22903
Phone: (804) 295-4333
Fax: (804) 295-2021
E-mail: 0246a@redroof.com
Page 130

Sprint
2211 Hydraulic Road
Charlottesville, Virginia 22901
Phone: (434) 971-2208
Fax: (434) 296-6417
E-mail: margaret.wright@mail.sprint.com
www.sprint.com
Pages 110-111

St. Anne's-Belfield School
2132 Ivy Road
Charlottesville, Virginia 22903
Phone: (434) 296-5106
Fax: (434) 979-1486
E-mail: admission@stab.org
www.stab.org
Pages 102-103

State Farm Insurance
1500 State Farm Boulevard.
Charlottesville, Virginia 22901
Phone: (434) 872-5000
Fax: (434) 872-5285
www.statefarm.com
Pages 134-135

Tandem Friends School
279 Tandem Friends School
Charlottesville, Virginia 22902
Phone: (434) 296-1303
Fax: (434) 296-1886
E-mail: toconnor@tandemfs.org
www.tandemfs.org
Page 105

Technicolor
P.O. Box 7427
Charlottesville, Virginia 22906
Phone: (434) 985-1100
Fax: (434) 985-9083
www.technicolor.com
Pages 116-117

University of Virginia
Charlottesville, Virginia 22904
Phone: (434) 924-0311
www.virginia.edu
Pages 98-101

**University of Virginia Community
Credit Union**
3300 Berkmar Drive
Charlottesville, Virginia 22901
Phone: (434) 964-2001
E-mail: contactus@uvaccu.com
www.uvacreditunion.org
Page 138

INDEX

■ ■ ■ ■ ■

Photo on 48-49 by Jeff Morgan appears with the permission of MIDWESTOCK

Photo on 50-51 by Michael Rush appears with the permission of MIDWESTOCK

Photo on 52 by John Mutrex appears with the permission of MIDWESTOCK

Photo on 66 by Novastock appears with the permission of MIDWESTOCK

Photos on 67 by Wally Emerson and Bill Bachmann appear with the permission of MIDWESTOCK

Photos on 68 and 69 Bill Bachmann appear permission of MIDWESTOCK

Photo on 107-108 by Michael Manheim appears permission of MIDWESTOCK

Photo on 142-143 by John Borge appears permission of MIDWESTOCK